ENEMIES OF PROSPERITY

HOW SOCIALISM, INTERVENTIONISM, AND THE WELFARE STATE MAKE US POOR AND UNFREE

Antony P. Mueller

Copyright © 2018 by Antony P. Mueller. All Rights Reserved.
ISBN: 9781731156983
All rights reserved. No part of this book may be reproduced in any form or by any electronic or mechanical means including information storage and retrieval systems, without permission in writing from the author. The only exception is by a reviewer and by academics, who may quote short excerpts in a review.
Printed in the United States of America

based on "Beyond the State and Politics. Capitalism for the New Millennium"
First Printing: April 2018
Amazon KDP
New edition July 2018
ISBN-9781980571445
also available as e-book

ENEMIES OF PROSPERITY

CONTENTS

Foreword
Introduction

    I.   The curse of socialism

A deadly utopia -
Command economy -
Backgrounder: Friedrich Hayek on central planning and totalitarianism -
Economic calculation -
Planned chaos - *Marxist errors* –
Backgrounder: Marx theory of the collapse of capitalism –
A dream becomes a nightmare -
Systemic Misery -
Summary

    II.   The fiasco of interventionism

The fiasco of interventionism
Fascist roots of interventionism -
Origins of modern state capitalism –
Rational irrationality -
Legacy of interventionism -
Backgrounder: Effects of price interventionism -
Interventionism and the market process -
Employment –
Power and economic law –

III.   Welfare: more costs than benefits

Healthcare costs –
Cost explosion in education -
Social policy –
Origins of social policy -
Missing standards –
The chimera of social justice –
Backgrounder: concepts of justice -

IV.   Perpetual fiscal and monetary crises

The economics of the public debt -
Where does the money come from? -
Capital, savings, and entrepreneurship -
Summary

Figures and Tables
Bibliographical references
About the author

INTRODUCTION

In the first two decades after the collapse of the Soviet Union and the fall of the Berlin Wall, warnings against a new wave of socialism would have seemed utterly unnecessary. Yet since about a decade ago, anti-capitalism is on the rise again and the socialist dream finds new followers. 'Social justice' is the battle cry of the new socialists who call themselves 'democratic'. Their call finds resonance with the so-called millennials.

The socialists claim they want equality and prosperity for all and one would achieve these goals by interventionism and the socialization of industry. But this assertion confounds the goal of socialism with the means. The Socialist leaders trick their followers into believing that the aim of socialism is equal to socialism as a method.

Because of failing to distinguish between socialism as an objective and socialism as a means, many people get deceived. They suppose that to achieve the socialist goal of equality and prosperity for all, one must install socialism as an economic system. Such a belief ignores the historical evidence which shows that the practice of socialism leads to the opposite of the expected prosperity. Instead of a better life, systemic misery is the consequence.

Socialism builds on the false identification of the objective with the means. The popularity of socialism comes from the illusion that goals and measures are identical and that because socialism is so good in its goals, socialism were just as preferable as a method. The right question to ask is how socialism can qualify as a means. Put this way, the answer becomes obvious: socialism as a means has failed on all counts. As Ludwig von Mises pointed out, the alternative between capitalism and socialism is not a choice between two social systems but between social cooperation and the disintegration of society.

A further device of socialist persuasion is the claim that socialism could cure social injustice and that injustice beyond socialism is universal. When one accepts the assertion of social injustice, there is no limit of the claims that society is obliged to heal the ailments one can bring forth in the name of the idea of social justice.

Because 'social justice' is a utopian concept, the social justice movement is so disruptive to society. Social justice is a hierarchical concept as it does not refer to the relation among equals but to a relationship of submission. Yet who is the suppressor? The society as a whole? The social justice movement works towards the disintegration of society. It is not a movement to achieve its declared aims, which is impossible, but to destroy them.

The social justice warriors promote specific groups and negate the principle of reciprocity as the foundation of society. They ignore that distributive justice cannot qualify as "a right." While the principle of reciprocal justice refers to the relationship of one person to another person and the procedural justice to the dispute resolution among dissenting individuals, social justice has not the individual at its core but the claims of groups against society. This logical contradiction makes 'social justice' a false construct.

'Social justice' is a notion that one can fill as one wishes with all kinds of demands. In the light of the ideal of social justice, injustice is universal. Once one takes up the endorsement of social justice, the Pandora's box is open for the exigency that society is obliged to cure the plethora of the ailments one can bring forth in the name of the violation of rights to social justice.

"Social injustice" – once taken for granted – is the universal tool of indictment against the capitalist society. To ward off the false accusations by disproving their empirical contents, does not help much. The claims will persist. More effective is to refute the claim of universal injustice from the onset and reject the proposition as an empty concept void of meaning and beset with contradictions.

In the debates to come, the defenders of prosperity and freedom must vigorously unmask the socialists' tricky confusion between goals and means. One must cull the allegation that social justice could form the basis of a legitimate entitlement.

The inequality of income and wealth in capitalism as an injustice is a constant point of accusation of the socialists. Marx misunderstood the essence of inequality in a market economy and put the capitalist property into the same category as wealth holds under feudalism. Marx did not recognize that the market process creates inequality because the failed projects vanish.

The socialists see those who have accumulated a fortune. They lament the inequality and ignore the fact that the capitalist process is an elimination process that roots out the losers of the game. In a competitive market economy, the expression 'successful entrepreneur' represents a pleonasm because businessmen who have no success are forced to leave and must make room for those entrepreneurs who better serve their customers.

The market competition works as a continuous process of correcting errors. Under market competition, only the successful entrepreneurs, those who master the challenges of satisfying the wants of the customers, will remain in business. Failed businesses must disappear. Bankruptcies make capitalism productive and are a sign that the markets function. In the reality of the market economy, the Marxist construct of a 'capitalist class' does not exist because each member must struggle for his membership every day and under free capitalism, both the entry and the exit doors are wide open.

The inequality in capitalism is the result of an elimination process. The failed entrepreneurs disappear from the market together with their projects and their associated firms.

Socialists denounce capitalism as a 'profit economy'. They indict making profits as the prime secular sin. By ignoring loss as the counterpart of profit, the socialist misjudge the role of profit in a market economy. Profit and loss, which arise from the difference between sales and costs, inform the business owner about the profitability of the company. If profit and loss disappear, the indicator of how well production serves the consumers vanishes with it. Without such signals, production takes place by happenstance and production may cost more than the goods are worth. Therefore, the production in socialist economies absorbs more material and human resources than the result will generate in utility. The lamented 'exploitation' of human labor, which socialist blame to exist in capitalism, is the systematic reality under socialism.

In the Soviet efforts to industrialize Russia, this negative-sum economy of socialism cost a colossal toll in human lives and labor. In the second decade of the new millennium, this exploitation of the masses continuous in Cuba, North Korea, and Venezuela. Karl Marx accused the market economy of the anarchy of production, yet it is, in fact, the socialist economic system, which suffers from chaos.

Planners can provide schemes to produce consumers goods based on surveys of the conditions among the population. For example, planners could try to determine how many pairs of shoes the population needs. Yet the planners cannot achieve these goals because they have no reliable and detailed knowledge about what consumers want but also do not have the guidelines as to the costs that producing the shoes would absorb in relation to satisfy urgent consumer wants, such as clothing, housing, and food.

In a market economy, the solution to this problem lies not in the hands of one central planning authority, but all market participants cooperate in the assessment process and delegate the production of the goods to different entrepreneurial units according to the specific capabilities of these individual companies that the market competition reveals. Each individual consumer expresses his subjective valuation in the act of purchase. The prices and the sold quantities are signals and incentives.

In a capitalist market economy, the owners of the means of production are involved at each stage of the production process to solve the valuation problem. But in the end, the valuation of the *consumers* determines the value of the capital that is employed in the production process.

The new "democratic socialists" want to make their followers believe that one could redistribute wealth and income and socialize a large part of the economy without harming production and productivity. They claim that a comprehensive control of the economy by the government would bring more justice and more prosperity. The democratic socialists want more planning and less market. Yet this postulate ignores that socialism does not fail by accident or circumstance.

Socialism suffers from four fundamental design defects. Each one of them is sufficient to make socialism inoperative.

Socialism eradicates private property and markets and thus eliminates effective economic coordination.

Second, the socialist organization of the economy allows soft budgets, which means that there is no mechanism in place that discards inefficient production units.

Third, the abolition of private property and the cult of the state promotes false incentives.

Finally, the socialist system with the absence of private property and of free markets inhibits rational economic calculation.

While socialism brings misery, distress, suppression of freedom, and a broken economy, this obvious failure of socialism does not quench the craving of the anti-capitalists to condemn the market economy. The critics denounce capitalism because it does not bring a paradise and because markets are not 'perfect' according to their imagination. The desire for the impossible is the reason for the popularity of the 'Third Way'. It promises a system beyond capitalism and socialism with the claim the best of the two worlds would merge.

Interventionism is the so-called Third Way, an economic system between capitalism and socialism. This economic regime comes along with political populism and results in state capitalism and the growth of government. People like to praise this mixed system as a welfare state, but they fail to recognize that this kind of governance does not lead to the hoped-for Eldorado but is the path to stagnation.

The welfare state produces most of the social ailments, which the government claims to heal. The more generous the social assistance, the larger the number of social welfare recipients, the higher the burden of the social tax contributions, and the more the shadow economy will flourish. More complicated the tax code, more tax evasion takes place. The more access to public healthcare and medication, the sicker people become. The higher the percentage of a populational cohort that attends high schools and colleges, the lower the educational level.

Interventionism hampers the dynamics of the markets and falsifies the price system. The administrative state perverts the market economy and reduces the effectiveness of the market as a coordination mechanism. The economic system gets weaker. Interventionism discourages innovation and leads to a waste of resources due to the cost of regulation and the misallocation brought about by the state intervention.

The results are perpetual fiscal and monetary crises.

I.
THE CURSE OF SOCIALISM

"Socialism is the fantastic younger brother of the despised despotism, which it wishes to inherit; its endeavors are thus, in the deepest sense, reactionary. For it desires an abundance of the power of the state, as only the despotism has had, and indeed it surpasses all the past by striving for the formal annihilation of the individual."
Friedrich Nietzsche: "Human, All Too Human", Chapter 10. Item Eight "A Look at the State" (1878)

- A deadly utopia
- Command economy

- *Backgrounder: Friedrich Hayek on central planning and totalitarianism*
- *Economic calculation*
- *Planned chaos*
- *Marxist errors*
- *Backgrounder: Marx's' theory of the collapse of capitalism*
- *A dream becomes a nightmare*
- *Systemic Misery*
- *Summary*

Socialism promises equality and that everyone would receive what he needs -whether one adds little or nothing to produce the goods. According to the socialist ideology, this promise, however, is not an invitation to parasitism since, according to the socialist thesis, a 'new man' would emerge in the socialist community. Instead of the capitalist egoist, a new creature would rise under socialism, someone whose prime attitude is altruism and universal benevolence. According to the socialist utopia, only those people would ask for assistance who truly need help while all other individuals would contribute as much as possible to produce the goods and services for the community. The socialist dream says that under socialism, there would be both: abundance and equality.

There is no end to discussing such possibilities. Yet the real problem why socialism cannot work is not because of ethics, but that under a socialist regime rational economic calculation is not feasible. Even if the promised 'new man' would have appeared and a new human creature would have come into being - socialism would fail. The problem of socialism is not egoism versus altruism but that it is impossible to calculate in a rational way how to produce. Because there are no money prices, no markets, and no private property, socialist economies cannot properly function. Instead of abundance, there is misery and instead of equality, there is suppression in socialism.

Socialism, when put into practice, leads to a command economy. In as much as some command and others must follow, equality ends. Where there is no private property, the state must determine the use of the goods through orders and commandos. Freedom vanishes and productivity sinks. This fate becomes already visible before full socialism has arrived.

Each step closer to socialism brings less productivity, less income, and less wealth. The idea of 'society as a whole' is an absurd concept. When production is 'socialized', it is not the 'society' that decides what to produce, how, and for whom, but a band of commissars. When there are no markets and no prices to guide economic decisions, the commissars will have to threaten and apply physical force to get their plans implemented.

A DEADLY UTOPIA

As soon as the Communists conquered the power in Russia in 1917, the new rulers established an oppressive apparatus, which grew into horrendous proportions. During the compulsory collectivization of agriculture, in the early 1920s and in further waves in the late 1920s and the early 1930s, the so-called 'Holodomor' cost the lives of millions of people who died due to executions, deportations, and famine. The human tragedy happened again in Communist China when Mao Zedong (1893-1976) prescribed the 'great leap forward' from 1958 to 1961.

A real abyss appears when one considers that National Socialism is socialism. As it says in its name, 'National Socialism' (Nazism) is the national version of socialism, while Soviet Communism is the international variant of socialism. Communist terror, however, came before the National Socialist era. In many respects, National Socialism was a reaction to international socialism. The Holodomor happened at the doorstep of Western Europe. The horrors of collectivization and the slaughtering of innocents by the Communist terror machine drove many people into the hands of Nazism and Fascism.

Table 1
State Murders by Socialist Regimes 1917-1979

REGIME	VICTIMS	PERIOD
Russian Soviet Communism	62 million	1917-1987
Chinese Communism	35 million	1949-1987
National Socialism	21 million	1933-1945
Cambodian Communism	2.0 million	1975-1979
North Korean Communism	1.7 million	1948-1987
Polish Communism	1.6 million	1945-1948
TOTAL	123.3 million	1917-1979

Figures are the average between the highest and the lowest estimate Source: R. J. Rummel, Death by Government, Transaction Publisher 1997

Website: https://www.hawaii.edu/powerkills/NOTE1.HTM

ENEMIES OF PROSPERITY

The term 'state murder' – 'democide' – refers to mass murders carried out by the force of state apart from wars. Elimination of its own citizens is the stamp of socialism. In a command economy, anyone who opposes the state becomes an enemy of the people. As it is impossible to obey the dictates of the command economy in its entirety, and as non-compliance counts as sabotage, one persecution wave follows the other.

It was the declared goal of the Soviet power to establish Communism on a worldwide scale through a world revolution. Germany was the number one on the list of countries to include in the Communist power range. The leading Communists (Leo Trotsky: 'What Next? Vital Questions for the German Proletariat'. January 1932) knew well that who owns Europe, owns the world, and that who owns Germany, owns Europe. At the beginning of the thirties, the leftist German Social Democratic Party, together with the Communist Party, gained more than half of the votes in the general election. That Germany would become Communist and thus surrender to the Soviet rule seemed a matter of time. While the Communist coups had failed at the end of World War I in 1919 in Bavaria, some other German States, and in various parts of Eastern Europe, a Communist takeover seemed inescapable in the early 1930s when the Great Depression raged.

In March 1919, leading members of the Russian Communist Party founded the Communist International (Comintern). The aim of this organization was to establish Communism in Europe and then in the world. The plan was to fight 'with all available means, including the armed forces, for the overthrow of the international bourgeoisie and to establish an international Soviet republic'. For a political party to join the Communist International under the leadership of the Soviet Communists, twenty-one conditions were necessary to comply with, among them

- to lead truly Communist propaganda and agitation and to preserve the idea of a dictatorship of the proletariat;
- remove all reformists from the responsible posts;
- in addition to the legal, create an illegal organization for subversive work.

***

States are fatal – not only for its foreign enemies but also for its own citizens. The rule holds that the more comprehensive the rule of the state and the more totalitarian its ideology, the more destructive is this state for its citizens. Since the socialist state is totalitarian, socialism is a regime that carries out mass murders.

If a socialist world government would come into existence, the known historical dimensions of killings would dwarf before the new potential of terror. Although under such a world socialist regime, there would be no more wars in the conventional sense, the democide – the killing of one's own citizens by such a world government – would ravage without restraint. 'World peace' under a socialist global government would eliminate international wars at the cost of an all-encompassing terror regime and an everlasting civil war. The way to prevent such a catastrophe demands to limit the role of state and politics wherever one can and oppose all plans of a world government. The libertarian agenda includes abolishing international institutions such as the United Nations, the International Monetary Fund, the World Bank, the World Climate Conference, and all the rest of the plethora of international institutions and organizations because they are the springboard of a world government.

In socialism, everything becomes a question of political power, not only the economy. Politics is the magnet that attracts those who seek dominance. The relentless pursuit of control over other people is a psychological trait common to all leaders in all political parties. Because of the overriding role of politics in a socialist system, everything in this society is subject to the vicissitudes of the power play.

A socialist system requires hierarchical command structures. Under the socialist rule, the 'new man' promised by the ideology comes into existence not as an angel but as an apparatchik and underling. The 'dictatorship of the proletariat' becomes a reality - not as an egalitarian rule but as a military regime. Deception and trickery rule everyday life in socialism. The system compels the individual to lie and to cheat systematically to survive.

Once the socialist regime is established, idealism vanishes, and the promised altruism makes way to crude selfishness. The dream becomes a nightmare. The revolutionaries turn into bureaucrats who block the attempts to transform the system since a change would put their position of power at risk. This lack of adaptability continues from the top down to the lower ranks and spreads throughout the economy and includes the cultural life. Together with the state, the economy falters and comes to a standstill. Culture becomes as blunt and drab as the socialist nightlife. After the decline follows stagnation. At the end of this process, a society emerges in which the military along with the Communist Party become the dominant institutions to rule over a corpse-like society and economy.

The rule of the socialist command economy begins by abolishing the price system and by doing away with the private ownership of the means of production. A war economy and military rule replace the market system. If socialism were to rule the world, it would lead to a global economic stagnation and to a worldwide decline. World socialism would mean global dictatorship based on a system of comprehensive military rule. This horror would happen without intention, due to the logic of a socialist system. Under the conditions of world communism, the population would become impoverished and suppressed and the opponents of the regime would suffer constant persecution and perish in camps or get killed right away.

Only in so far as there is space for a market-based commerce, a socialist system can somewhat still work. That Soviet communism could last from 1917 to 1991 is because that in Russia and in the countries dominated by the Soviets, the market economy was not fully eliminated and that these countries did not cut themselves off from the capitalist environment. Under a system of global Communism, however, it would no longer be possible to find orientation by imitating the price system of the capitalist countries. Then, the economy would be on the brink of total collapse and the regime could only sustain itself through the unremitting application of brutal force. The victory of world communism would surpass any known historical dimensions of terror and misery. Yet this was the plan that lay at the foundation of the Soviet Union and at the Communist plans of a world revolution.

From the inception of the Soviet rule onwards, the Soviet economy existed as a war economy. Until the beginning of World War II, the Red Army waged wars against Poland (1919-21 and 1939), the Baltic countries (1918-20), Finland (1939), and Japan (1939). The Red Army invaded Poland in 1939 and took its share of the country's Eastern part in an accord with Nazi Germany that grabbed the Western part of Poland. The Red Army waged the civil war (1917-1922) against the White Army and carried out the forced collectivization of agriculture with military force at the end of the 1920s into the 1930s. The Soviet economy developed as a war economy and remained one until the end of the Soviet Union on December 26, 1991.

The Soviet Union existed as 13 military districts. The Soviet army relied on conscription for its personnel. Together with a huge contingent of female soldiers, the Soviet Union could mobilize over ten million soldiers. The construction of large factories had already begun in the 1920s to produce attack-capable weaponry. By the 1930s, the Soviet Union had the most advanced paratrooper army ready to invade its neighboring countries and to go beyond. In 1941, the Soviet Union had thousands of tanks, more than all other armies combined and four times as many as Nazi Germany.

While the mass of the population in Soviet Russia lived in poverty and without freedom, Soviet Communism established itself as a powerful militarist regime. After the Soviet Union came into existence, the Soviet Communist Party became the leader of the Communist world. Using the military counted as a legitimate means to conquer the world and put it under Communist rule. The purpose of taking power in Russia was not to liberate the Russian people from the oppressive Tsarist rule but the Communist revolution was to serve as the first step on the road to world revolution and global dominance.

The history of the Soviet Union is a history of murder waves. Already on the way to establishing the Soviet power in the civil war, millions of people had to let their lives. Introducing socialist production forms in the new Soviet territory required further millions of victims, and the collectivization of agriculture from 1929 cost the life of over ten million people. The victims of the Soviet class warfare were not only 'capitalists', but prominent intellectuals, the priests of the Orthodox church, millions of common people, and all anti-Communists.

Even during World War II, the democide did not cease. Without counting the victims of war, 13 million people lost their lives - among them 10 million Soviet citizens - during the war. After the Second World War, the murders continued, and the Soviet regime engineered a further 15 million victims.

Table 2
Democides by the Soviet regime

PERIOD	VICTIMS (in millions)	YEAR OF INCEPTION
Civil War	3.3	1917
New Economic Policy	2.2	1923
Collectivization	11.4	1929
The Great Terror	4.4	1936
Pre-World War II	5.1	1939
World War II	13.1	1941
Post-World War II	15.6	1946
Post-Stalin Era	6.9	1954
Total	61.9	1917

Source: Rummel, R.J.: Lethal Politics: Soviet Genocide and Mass Murder Since 1917. New Brunswick, N.J.: Transaction Publishers, 1990, Table 1.1. https://www.hawaii.edu/powerkills/USSR.TAB1.1.GIF

After the fall of the Soviet Union, the new accessible KGB documents revealed that from 1929 to 1953 some 28 million people fell victim to deportations and forced labor in the GULAG and that millions perished in the Holodomor of the 1930s. (For more details see Yuri Maltsev: Mass Murder and Public Slavery: The Soviet Experience. The Independent Review. Fall 2017). For the development of the Soviet Economy see: Peter Boettke: The Political Economy of Soviet Socialism.

***

The Second World War merged into the Cold War so that the Soviet economy existed as a war economy also in the second half of the 20th century until the Soviet Union collapsed. The dominance of the military in a Communist state is not accidental as it is also evident in the two Communist states that still exist: North Korea and Cuba.

In its nationalist form, too, Socialism works as a war economy to the extent that the national economy serves for the war aims. National Socialism, like the Soviet Communism, is unsuitable to satisfy the variety of the consumers' wishes. As an economic system, socialism, be it nationalist or internationalist, functions as a war economy. As soon as the economic planners try to include consumers' preferences beyond the military requirements, production falters, and distribution becomes precarious. Be it Soviet Communism or National Socialism, socialism creates not prosperity but poverty and oppression.

COMMAND ECONOMY

In socialism, commandments rule and people must obey. Those who do not take part in the Communist Party must lead an existence at the margin. In as much as there is still supply of high-quality consumer goods, it is possible because socialist countries coexist with market economies and have some foreign trade. The Socialist planners could copy the price relations from the capitalist countries thus try to adapt their plans to these indications of scarcity. Without such price signals, the socialist economic leaders would lose orientation about the costs of the input factors of production. Beyond market prices, there are no gauges with which amount and kind of capital goods and by how much work one should produce a commodity - and be it only a pencil or a cooker. Socialism means economic blindness. The price tag disappears, and so both, the consumers and the planners, lose informational orientation about rational economic conduct.

Socialists suppose that to implant their rule all that is necessary is to socialize the private companies, replace the management, and install workers councils, and the new economic order would flourish. The socialists ignore that the socialization of the means of production is just a beginning. What matters is how to run a business.

The planners may know what type of technology a specific production would require, and they can count on the professionalism of the engineers to use their knowledge. The error of socialist economic planning, however, lies in believing that business management could also continue as before after socialist operators take over the capitalist management. While the socialist regime can train administrators and engineers, and put the party members in leadership positions, these new leaders cannot decide according to relative scarcities because there is no longer a private property-based entrepreneurial price system available.

Many supporters of socialism believe business management is nothing more than a kind of registration or simple bookkeeping. Vladimir Ilyich Lenin (1870-1924), the Soviet revolutionary leader, believed that for the conduct of business operations the knowledge of reading and writing, as well as some expertise in the use of the four basic arithmetic operations and some training in accounting, would be enough to manage a company. The socialists then and now ignore the fundamental economic problem, which consists in determining what to produce, for whom, and how. The socialist planners assume that a plan can stipulate these three tasks and ignore how and where such a plan should find its standard of valuation. The basic error of the socialists is the presumption that one could manage a complex economy without capitalists and entrepreneurs.

Even if, for example, the plan should stipulate to produce a certain number of pencils for the literacy campaign, and that the order would go to the respective factories, the question arises how to design and by which combination of the factors of production the manufacturing should take place. When prices and markets disappear, one loses the orientation about which factors of production are more and which are less scarce along with the loss of knowledge of the costs of the goods used in the production process.

Scarcity makes goods valuable, and that something is valuable, expresses itself in its higher relative price in the market economy. Observing the prices, the market participants receive information about scarcity and align their economic decisions to the market signals. Yet when there is no market, information about the relation between the wants for goods and their supply vanishes. In a market economy, the economic participants need only partial knowledge to act rationally.

The price system informs about the scarcity relation and makes it possible to decide according to one's own best interests. There is no need for comprehensive information since markets enable to weigh the advantages and disadvantages of economic actions by way of the relative prices because the price system reduces complexity for the individual decision maker to the single number of the price.

In socialism, however, private ownership of the means of production no longer exists, and thus there is no price system for capital goods available. Institutionally, socialism consists in abolishing the market economy and replacing it with a planned economy. Yet beyond the loss of private property, the fundamental problem comes from the consequence that by doing away with private property of the means of production, one wipes-out information as well. Even if prices for consumer goods continue to exist, and if there is private ownership of consumer goods, the orientation about the relative scarcity of capital goods is lost as the socialist system removes the private ownership of the production goods and eliminates the role of the entrepreneur.

> **Friedrich Hayek on central planning and totalitarianism**
>
> "The reasons why the adoption of a system of central planning necessarily produces a totalitarian system are fairly simple. Whoever controls the means must decide which ends they are to serve. As under modern conditions control of economic activity means control of the material means for practically all our ends, it means control over nearly all our activities. The nature of the detailed scale of values which must guide the planning makes it impossible that it should be determined by anything like democratic means. The director of the planned system would have to impose his scale of values, his hierarchy of ends, which, if it is to be sufficient to determine the plan, must include a definite order of rank in which the status of each person is laid down. If the plan is to succeed or the planner to appear successful, the people must be made to believe that the objectives chosen are the right ones. Every criticism of the plan or the ideology underlying it must be treated as sabotage. There can be no freedom of thought, no freedom of the Press, where it is necessary that everything should be governed by a single system of thought. In theory, Socialism may wish to enhance freedom, but in practice, every kind of collectivism consistently carried thought must produce the characteristic features which Fascism, Nazism, and Communism have in common. Totalitarianism is nothing but consistent collectivism, the ruthless execution of the principle that 'the whole comes before the individual' and the direction of all members of society by a single will supposed to represent the 'whole'."
>
> (Friedrich A. Hayek, 1941, p. 583 in: "Planning, Science and Freedom", Nature 148 (15 November 1941), also available as "Planning, Science, and Freedom," Mises Daily (Auburn, AL: The Ludwig von Mises Institute, 27 September 2010)

Organization of the planned economy

The management plan in socialism shows a hierarchical structure of the command path from top to bottom (by way of commandos and force) and the information obligation from bottom to top (confirmation of the execution of the order). The consumer appears in the system only at the margin.

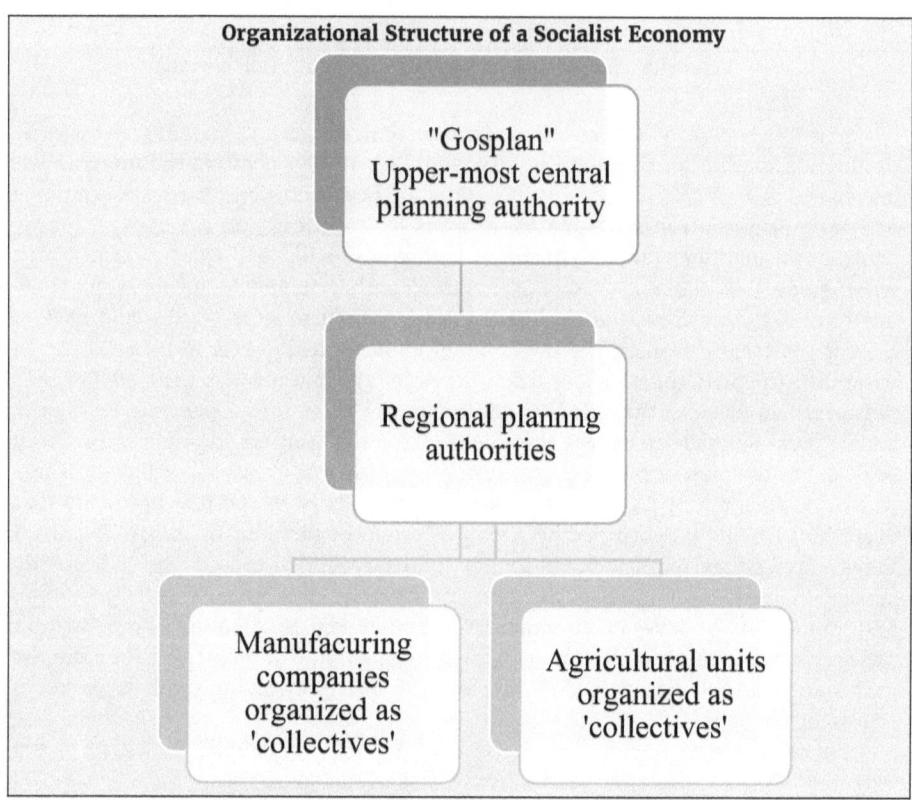

The socialist economy does not serve the consumers. The point of reference for proper management is to execute the commands – the same as in the military. To fulfill plans refers to the respective level in the hierarchy of the command order – not to the consumer.

Production faces the problems that there is an almost unlimited number of ways how to produce a good. One can manufacture a commodity with very different raw materials, technologies, and combinations of the production factors. The industrial feasibility and its technical optimum can only give a partial sign since many ways of construction are possible.

Before the aspects of technological feasibility could be considered, producing a good requires applying economic principles – the calculation of its potential profitability. Without cost calculation in relation to sales, a technical evaluation makes no sense. What is technically possible is not economically recommended, and what appears optimal from a technical point of view need not be so in terms of profits. With costs left out of consideration, socialist production is blind to the risk of producing goods that would cost more than they are worth. Who determines value? In a market economy, it is the client, and, in the last instance, the consumer.

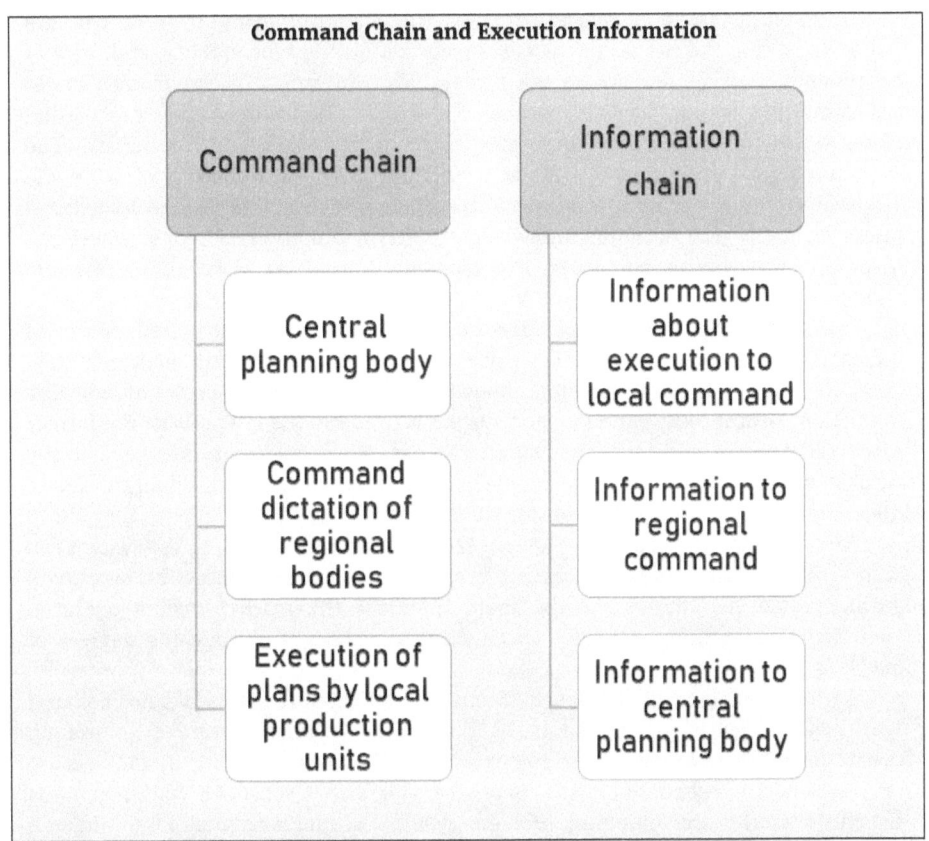

In central planning economy, it is up to the planners to determine the value. This, however, they cannot accomplish because preferences and technologies change, and the complexity of the relationship among the goods exceeds the capacity of anyone's mind or that of a planning committee to grasp.

Without a price system, the constructors of a product cannot know whether the resources the plan foresees to use are in demand to produce other goods that may be more urgent. In the market economy, the price is the signal whether a certain commodity is scarce or abundant. If a good is expensive, it shows that many other economic agents also want to use this product or the resources that one needs to produce this commodity. The market price expresses the prevailing socio-economic conditions. Socialism means economic blindness. Information is lost along with the incentive to act according to the price signals. In capitalism, the motivations of gaining profits and to avoid costs work as an incentive to behave rationally. In a market economy, the prices fulfill the double function to inform and to incentivize the producer and the buyer.

Capitalism is a system in which the higher profits come to those who are best at satisfying the wishes of the customers concerning type, quality, and price of the product. Even if one would want to satisfy the wants of the masses under socialism, this is not possible because the system has purged the information necessary to do. Socialism eliminates both: information and incentives. The economic actors must operate in the dark. They may have a sense of what the consumers might want and may want to produce it, but this diffuse knowledge differs from the way economic knowledge exists in a market economy, where the prices and the acts of purchases of a company's products show the customers' willingness to pay by the penny and the result appears as profit and loss.

At the beginning of socialization, the planners may still find points of orientation in the former capitalist price conditions. The socialist managers then come to grips with this residual knowledge in the early stages of socialist production. Yet the longer the socialist system is in place, the less reliable the former price relations to guide the production process. The conditions change, but the socialist steering apparatus has no mechanism to register these changes and to implement this knowledge. The longer the socialists are ruling, the more they shove the economy into misallocation. The longer socialism exists, the less the system can learn - opposite to a market economy, in which the economic actors become more knowledgeable the longer and the more intensive the market system operates. Capitalism is a learning system - socialism is a system of diminishing degrees of knowledge.

The socialism of the Soviet Union and its satellite states did not collapse right away because the remnants of the market economy were still around, international trade with capitalist countries was not completely cut off, and because a private shadow economy existed. If one considers that socialism will encompass the entire world, the planning problem would become overwhelming. Under a worldwide communist regime, the planning authority would create an uncoordinated economy. Such a system would deal lavishly with scarce resources but ignore abundant resources. The system would generate vast misallocations. Of some commodities, too many would be produced, while other more urgent goods would be in short supply. Not the actual demand would count but the vicissitudes of the production plans. As a result, goods would be of bad quality and very costly relative to the wage level.

Under a global socialism, the economies would fall into deep misery even more so than it is already the case under a single socialist economy. A global socialist system would descend into an economic abyss even if at the beginning it would seem as if the opposite were to happen when the wealth that had been accumulated by the capitalist economic order serves for the promised 'just' distribution.

ECONOMIC CALCULATION

As early as in 1922, five years after the Communist takeover in Russia, Ludwig von Mises (1881-1973) wrote his profound analysis of the consequences of the lack of economic calculation in the socialist economy. Mises' approach was novel because he showed that the fundamental problem of a socialist economy is not a moral one but an economic issue. Without a price system and property rights, the economic entities lose the basis of calculation and thus of rational economic conduct.

In a market economy, the relative prices of the goods serve as a guide for the proper economic action. These price ratios reflect the combination of the production factors that best satisfy consumers' needs. Relative prices show what consumers want and guide the production process into this direction because this is where the profits emerge. The competition provides the incentives for cost-effectiveness so that consumers receive the goods at the lowest prices based on the best use of the factors of production.

In capitalism, the wishes of the clients determine the overall structure of the price relations. The preferences of the consumers determine also the values of the investment goods. This imputation of the value estimation goes from the consumers to the value of the production goods. It takes place according to the contribution of the investment goods to the value of the final consumption good that is produced by the capital good. The value of the final product determines the value of the intermediate goods. The anchor for the value structure of the entire wealth in a market economy is the final use of the goods by the consumer.

Under capitalism, it is not a planning authority that controls the production structure, but the consumers decide. These control the economy because only those entrepreneurs that obey the calls of the consumers can gain an extra profit. In a capitalist economy, the production follows the wishes of the consumers. Businesses must restructure the production according to the changes of consumer wants, needs and tastes. Therefore, business management is not an uncomplicated undertaking as Lenin had presumed.

Production direction and value creation

The expected prices of the consumer goods determine the prices of the investment goods.

The costs of capital goods do not determine the value of the consumer goods, but the value of the consumer goods determines the value of the production goods that is used producing the consumer goods.

The direction of valuation of the value of capital goods runs from the value of consumer goods to capital goods while the direction of the production process in time runs from the early stages of production to the present.

Time directions of production and valuation

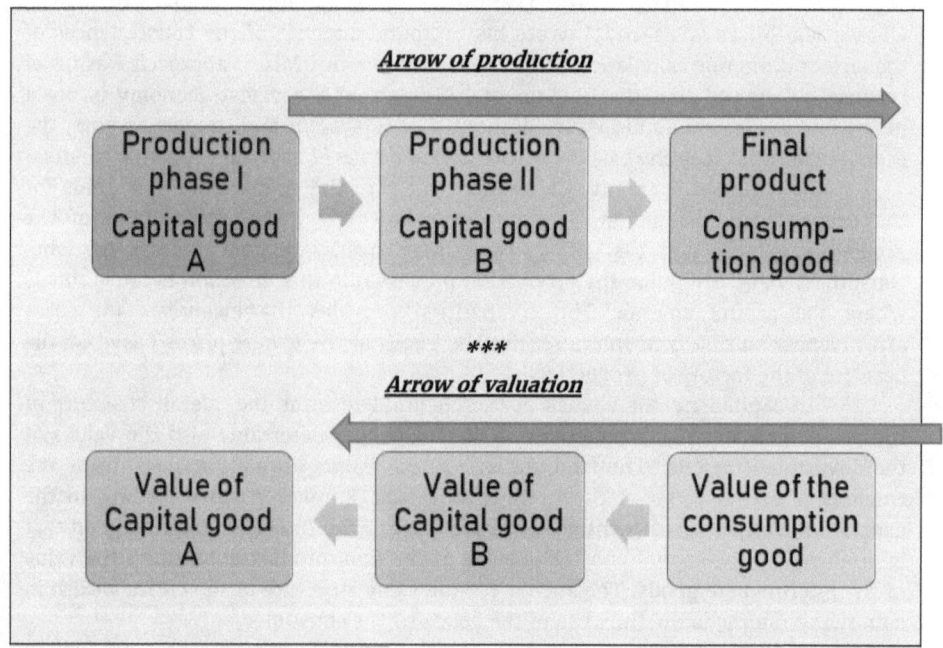

The capitalist mode of production uses market prices, which result from the interplay of individual subjective estimates of subjective utility to assess the value of capital goods in this process.

Market prices objectively indicate how wants are distributed in society in terms of the economic actors' willingness to pay.

***

Ludwig von Mises shows in his analysis of the economy under socialism that a private property-based pricing system must be available to evaluate the goods used in production. The price is objective in the sense as it bundles the various subjective valuations present in the society. The values of the consumption goods depend on the wishes of the consumers as they reveal their wants by their willingness to pay. The link between the value of a consumer good and a capital good becomes clear when the production process moves closer to the end of the production chain. The further away from consumption that the capital good stands in the time order of the production structure, the less does the subjective valuation of the consumer goods determine the value of the production good. Without a price system, no individual and no expert planning team, no matter how excellent, could survey and appraise the almost endless variety of combinations in the production process.

In order to gain an orientation in this maze, one needs price ratios, which reflect the exchange conditions on the market. It is the function of entrepreneurs to appraise these price ratios and to make business decisions. The more extensive the market, and the more intensive the competition, the more and the better the information input in the system.

There are also socialized enterprises in a market economy system. However, these state enterprises, including municipal enterprises, can behave economically when they follow the guidance of the private price system of the capitalist environment. This is possible if the market economy is still the dominant system. The same applies to the socialist economies when they use international prices from the capitalist countries. In the system of global socialism, however, these points of reference are no longer present. The planners are then unaware of the conditions of scarcity.

As Mises explains in his essay on economic calculation under socialism, any economic endeavor "becomes a feat whose success can neither be estimated in advance nor can it be evaluated later in retrospect ... Socialism is the abolition of the rationality of the economy". Only the monetary calculation of business based on prices offers a guide through the "overwhelming abundance of economic possibilities". Without the calculation of prices by means of money, "all production with far-reaching processes would be a tapping in the dark." (Ludwig von Mises: Economic Calculation in the Socialist Commonwealth)

The value of an investment project does not follow from its cost but from the extent to which the investment contributes to satisfying the subjective utility of the consumer. Due to this connection between value and price, the entrepreneur will gain the information whether it is worthwhile to bear the costs of a project or to refrain from its realization. The cost calculation is an indispensable tool for estimating the profit chances of a project, yet the final judgment about the profits is in the hands of the consumers according to their willingness to pay a price. This also applies to investment goods, which have value only in as much as they contribute to producing consumables. The entrepreneurial contribution to each production stage along the production chain will get its final financial compensation only when the consumers have paid the goods.

From an economic point of view, the entrepreneur must fulfill two functions: first, estimate the future wants of the buyer and, second, produce these goods at the minimum cost. These tasks require experimentation. Trial and error lie at the heart of the market-based competition process. If there is no competition, the companies lose both the orientation what consumers want and about how to manufacture the goods in a cost-efficient way. Even if the socialist planners wanted the best for the consumers, they could not determine the optimal production structure because they do not have the information of the market prices about the degree of the prevalent degrees of scarcity.

Socialism as an economic system had already failed in the early phase of the Soviet Union. The Soviet economy survived as a war economy. The main purpose of the economic activity was to serve the needs of the military. The wishes of the consumers found only marginal consideration. It would be wrong, however, to conclude that the Soviet economy could not be a consumer economy because the Soviet Union was compelled to give priority to the military. The war economy was the only way that the Soviet planned economy could at least somewhat function.

Why socialism cannot work

Socialism suffers from four defects. Each one of these would be sufficient to make socialism inoperative.

Socialism eradicates private property and markets and thus eliminates rational calculation and effective coordination.

Additionally, it allows soft budgets, which means that there is no mechanism in place that discards inefficient production units.

Thirdly, the abolition of private property and the cult of the state promotes false incentives.

Finally, the socialist system with the absence of private property and of free markets inhibits rational economic calculation.

Design Defects of Socialism

Impossibility of rational calculation (absence of private property and abolition of markets)	**Impossibility of effective economic coordination** (elimination of free price system)
False incentives (abolition of private property and the cult of the state)	**Soft budgets – ineffective elimination of unproductive units** (absence of profit and loss calculation)

Construction & Design Defects of Socialism

PLANNED CHAOS

Socialists accuse the market economy of the anarchy of production, yet it is, in fact, the socialist economic system, which suffers from chaos. Scarcity requires economic behavior. Prices indicate the relative availability of a good. Profit and loss, which arise from the difference between sales and costs, inform the business owner about the profitability of the company. If profit and loss disappear under socialism, the indicator of how well production serves the consumers also vanishes. Without such signals, production takes place by happenstance and production may cost more than the goods are worth for the final user. The socialist economy absorbs more material and human resources than the production generates in utility. The lamented 'exploitation' of human labor, which socialist blame to exist in capitalism, is the systematic reality under socialism. This negative-sum economy of socialism cost a colossal toll in human lives and labor in the Soviet efforts to industrialize Russia. In the second decade of the new millennium, this exploration of the masses continuous in Cuba, North Korea, and Venezuela.

Planners can provide schemes to produce consumers goods based on surveys of the conditions among the population. For example, planners could try to determine how many pairs of shoes the population needs. Yet the planners cannot achieve these goals because they have no reliable and detailed knowledge about what consumers want but also do not have the guidelines as to the costs that producing the shoes would absorb in relation to satisfy urgent consumer wants, such as clothing, housing, and food. In a market economy, the solution to this problem lies not in the hands of one central planning authority, but all market participants cooperate in the assessment process and delegate the production of the goods to different entrepreneurial units according to the specific capabilities of these individual companies that the market competition reveals. Each individual consumer expresses his subjective valuation in the act of purchase. The prices and the sold quantities are signals and incentives. In a capitalist market economy, the owners of the means of production are involved at each stage of the production process to solve the valuation problem. In the end, the valuation of the consumers determines the value of the capital that is employed in the production process.

In socialism, however, workers and engineers work without entrepreneurship in the absence of the capitalists and of the capitalist managers. The socialists want to make the entrepreneurs superfluous and put the production apparatus into the hands of the workers and their leaders. The socialists believe that they can achieve a better economic performance through the socialization of the enterprises. The anti-capitalists come to this false idea because they do neither understand the function of the entrepreneur nor that of the capitalist.

Unlike the administrator, the entrepreneur represents the creative force of the business. The task of the entrepreneur – who may or may not be the owner or co-owner of a company – is to realize business ideas. The entrepreneur is the one looking for the best way to satisfy customers' wishes, how best to produce with the production equipment, and how best to organize the plant. An entrepreneur is someone who enforces these ideas. Different from the entrepreneur, the function of the capitalist is to maintain the capital structure. Capitalists finance the production process. They receive their compensation only with the sale of the final good while the workers receive their salaries already during the time of the production process. When the capitalists and the entrepreneurs disappear, and the socialists seize power, the capital structure disintegrates because there is no one left with a personal interest in financing and managing the edifice of capital with the final consumer in mind.

MARXIST ERRORS

Karl Marx (1818-1883) ignored the role played by the capitalist and entrepreneur in the market economy. Marx saw the capitalist as someone who, like it was the case with Marx' collaborator Friedrich Engels (1820-1895), owns a fortune and receives dividends and interest payments without an accomplishment of one's own. Biographers of the communist labor movement leader claim that Marx never saw a factory from within. Friedrich Engels, the financial sponsor of the Marxist project to conquer the world, was the heir of a fortune that his father had accumulated, and that the son would spend not only as a supporter of Karl Marx and the socialist movement but also as a playboy. Friedrich Engels was neither a capitalist nor an entrepreneur, but an inheritor and a parasite like Marx. Engels kept Karl Marx financially above water, particularly in the period after the socialist author had squandered the inheritance of his noble wife.

Marx and his successors ignore that the capitalists pre-finance and preserve the capital structure of the economy. Capital formation requires before everything else, abstention from using one's full potential of consumption. The capitalists are those who do this by financing the production processes until the commodity reaches the consumer as the finished product ready for use.

In order to understand the role of the capitalists in the market economy, one must consider that each product runs through a lengthy production process until it reaches the consumers. This production process extends from the planning process onward through the different processing stages until the goods get to the warehouses and the exhibition and sales rooms and includes the marketing to sell the goods. The receipts come only with the sale of the final good.

By the time when the capitalist receives income from the consumer, time passes, and the entire process is subject to risk and uncertainty. The capitalists receive their reward because of waiting and of bearing risks and uncertainties while the wage earners receive their remuneration regularly long before the product reaches the final consumer.

Under market competition, only the successful entrepreneurs and capitalists, those who master the challenges of satisfying the customers, will remain in business. The failed entrepreneurs disappear from the market together with their projects and their associated firms. The socialists see those who have accumulated a fortune. They lament the inequality and ignore the fact that the capitalist process is an elimination process that roots out the losers of the game.

The market process creates inequality because the failed projects vanish. The inequality in capitalism is the result of the elimination process, which is the reason why capitalism is so productive. The market competition forces the unsuccessful entrepreneurs to disappear and to make room for those who are better in satisfying the customer's wishes. In the reality of the market economy, the Marxist construct of a 'capitalist class' does not exist because each member must struggle for his membership every day and both the entry and the exit doors are wide open.

Backgrounder:
Marx' Theory of the Collapse of Capitalism

According to the Marxist doctrine, the characteristic feature of capitalism is that the use of money serves to produce goods to earn more money.

Marx put this idea in his 'formula' of M-G-M', which means that money (M) serves to produce goods (G) to earn more money (M').

In the Marxian model, the capitalist profits result from the exploitation of the workers because capitalists gain the surplus value, which the workers create. The surplus value depends on the so-called 'organic composition of the capital', which includes the 'constant capital' of machines and property and the 'variable capital', which represents the labor force in the production process.

Following Marx, the capitalist competition compels the companies to increase the constant capital. This reduces the relative share of the variable capital and the profitability of the capitalist firm falls since the extraction of the surplus value as the rate of exploitation depends on the relative size of labor in relation to constant capital.

'Das Kapital' Volume I was published in 1867. Volume II and III were published after the death of Karl Marx (1883) in 1885 and 1894 respectively.

The focal point of the Marxist model is the thesis that entrepreneurial profit results from the exploitation of the labor force and that in as much as the concentration of capital reduces the extraction of surplus value, profits will shrink, and capitalism will collapse.

For Marx, the solution is socialism as a system under which the workers retain that part of the work which capitalist extract as surplus value from the working proletariat.

The central problem of the Marxist model is the assumption that the value of a product is equal to the labor effort needed for its production. Marx took this error from the classical economists who already had noted its paradoxical implications and the clash of the labor theory of value with reality.

Only five years after Marx published the first volume of "Capital", the neoclassical revolution happened, which corrected the fundamental error of classical economics.

Neoclassical economic theory resolved the paradox of value. The neoclassical approach clarifies that the value of goods and services depends on the subjective valuation of the individual buyers and is determined not in terms of averages and totals but on the margin.

Marx' Concept of the Capitalist Crisis Cycle

Accumulation Phase

- Money - good - money (M-G-M') capitalists use money to earn money
- Capitalist competition compels the accumulation of physcial capital in the production process
- Increase of the 'organic compositon of capital' with the wage share sinking and the capital share rising

Collapse

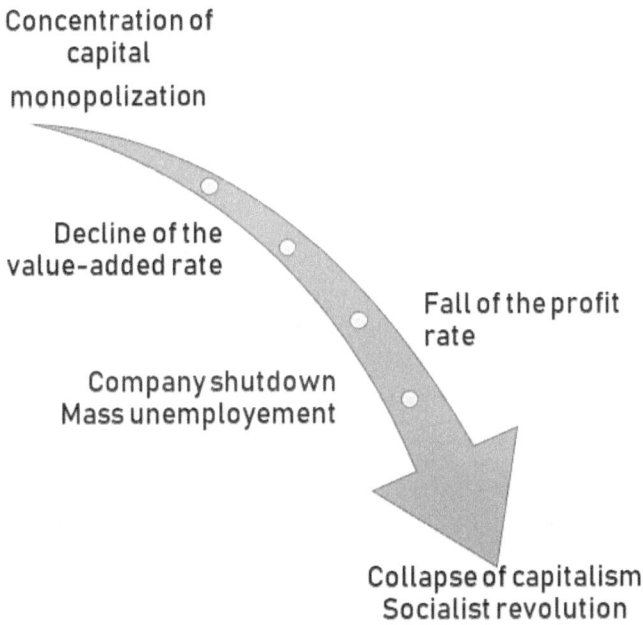

***

According to the Marxist doctrine, capitalism suffers from crises that become more severe and destructive over time, and finally, bring the complete collapse of capitalism. The capitalist competition leads to an army of unemployed persons and to the impoverishment of the working class and to a growing concentration of capital. According to this theory, the mass of the proletarians will grow, while the number of the capitalists will shrink. This theory concludes that to the extent that the volume of the active labor force falls in the production process, the profits will decrease and thereby capitalism brings about its own downfall.

Yet during the 150 years that have elapsed since 'Das Kapital' (1867) appeared in print, the opposite development has occurred:

Instead of mass impoverishment, a new middle class has emerged, and extreme poverty has decreased worldwide the more countries have turned to capitalism. Today, there are more companies than ever in the world, where profits expand production, to introduce technical progress, and to raise productivity and with it the wages.

A DREAM BECOMES A NIGHTMARE

Socialism demands the socialization of the means of production. Central management will replace the market. The original idea of Karl Marx was that socialism would lead to the death of the state. The opposite has happened.

Under no other form of economic production has the state become larger, stronger, more powerful, and more suppressive than under socialism. The internal contradictions of this economic system were soon recognized. This insight, however, did not bring the utopians to discard their dream into the dustbin of history, but rather the socialists ignored the criticism of their utopia. For the dream that the socialist way of production could work, idealist revolutionaries and the dictators who followed them sacrificed millions of people. While some of those who were in favor of socialism at the beginning of the movement may be dispensed of their error because of their inexperience, yet the socialists of today can no longer claim ignorance after the dimension of the brutal repression that came with the socialist system have become known.

Karl Marx, who opposed the socialist utopians, avoided answering the question how socialism would function. In his writings, he concentrated on the criticism of capitalism and he lost only a few words on how socialism may look like and how it could operate. Yet how far from reality the ideas about the future communist reality of Marx and Engels were, shows up in the following quotation. According to this Marx-Engels citation, it would be possible under communism "to do this today, to do that tomorrow, and to hunt in the morning, to fish in the afternoons, to breed cattle in the evening, to criticize after eating, without ever becoming a hunter, a fisherman, a shepherd, or a critic." (Marx-Engels-Werke, Vol. 3, Berlin 1969, p. 33). Apart from these promises, Marx did not much to elaborate the practical aspects of socialism. Instead, he would put forth the assertion of the historical inevitability of socialism. Marx took the postulate of historical necessity from his philosophical master G. W. F. Hegel (1770-1831) yet transported the Hegel's concept of the world spirit into economic history. What for Hegel was the path to freedom, became for Marx the road to bondage. The intellectual development towards liberty in the philosophy of Hegel turned into the deterministic historical materialism in the philosophy of Karl Marx.

According to the Marxist idea of the ultimate determination of the historical development, the march to the socialist rule can be slowed down or accelerated, but ultimately cannot be stopped. In the end, socialism will be victorious - the sooner the better. For the daily political struggle, this position meant that all opponents of socialism were reactionaries who prevent the socialist paradise from becoming the new heavenly reality now already. The postulate of the historical necessity of socialism implies that the socialist front as the leaders of the proletariat have the right and the obligation to eliminate those persons who resist the socialist movement because they postpone the coming of the socialist paradise. In the perspective of historical materialism, the predestined coming of the socialist paradise justifies and requires the physical removal of the opponents of socialism.

The supposedly scientific nature of historical materialism underpins the claim of determinism. This belief was effective when, in the middle of the nineteenth century, science had gained a religious status. The members of this new hybrid class of intellectuals who belong neither to the bourgeoisie nor to the nobility or to the working class had abandoned the traditional religious beliefs to assume a secular religion with as much fervor as they distanced themselves from the faith that they once held in childhood. The revolutionaries regarded religion as an obstacle to the unlimited progress that would come with socialism. Socialism and atheism were to be inseparable. With the claim of being scientific, the fantastic pronouncement of the utopia of a land of plenty for all finds its anchor in the belief of a heaven on earth.

As a child of his time, Marx was a naïve believer in science as determinism. Marxists assert that criticism of their theory is unscientific when, in fact, Marxism itself is unscientific as it sells a belief system as a proven theory. Since the times of Marx, the promoters of the socialist movement accuse anyone who turns against it as being an advocate of inequality, and as someone who does not want justice for the world but favors exploitation and inequality to continue.

The fusion of determinism and science with the promises of justice and happiness for all leads to a striking combination, which has been appealing to intellectuals. Up to the present day mainly academics believe in Marxism. Workers, after all, are a part of the economic reality of the production process and know that the socialist promises are rubbish. Nowhere has socialism established itself as the result of a workers' movement. The workers have never been the perpetrators of socialism but always its victim. The leaders of the revolution have been party politicians and military men. It was up to the intellectuals and artists to conceal the brutality of the socialist regimes through articles and books and by films, songs, and paintings, and to give socialism a scientific-intellectual, aesthetic and moral appearance. In the socialist propaganda, the new system appears to be both fair and productive.

While Marxism has disappeared from the workers' movement, Marxist theory flourishes today in culture, the academic world, and in the mass media. This 'cultural Marxism' goes back to Antonio Gramsci (1891-1937) and the Frankfurt School. The theorists of Marxism recognized that the proletariat would not play the expected historical role as a 'revolutionary subject'. Therefore, for the revolution to happen, the movement must depend on the cultural leaders to destroy the existing Christian culture and morality and then drive the disoriented masses to Communism as their new creed.

The final goal of this movement is to establish a world government in which the Marxist intellectuals have the say. The Russian Revolution was neither Russian nor proletarian. It had not come from a labor movement, but from a group of professional revolutionaries. A closer look at the personal composition of the Bolshevist party and the at first governments of the Soviet state and its repressive apparatus reveals the true character of the Soviet revolution as a project that did not aim at freeing the Russian people from the Tsarist joke but planned to launch a world revolution.

The supporters of socialism recognized that their preferred system could not function without a dictatorship. In order to succeed, the dictatorship must come in disguise, in the form of a mind control. For that purpose, the cultural Marxists postulate and exaggerate the role of social, sexual and racial differences. They play a game of confusion by promulgating that socialism can be democratic and that true communism has not yet existed but was to come - all the while calling themselves 'liberals' to usurp a label that connotes freedom.

When the murderous reality of communism in the Soviet system became known, the term 'communism' fell out of favor and was replaced by the less burdened concept of 'socialism'. When the concept of 'socialism' became less radiant, the expression 'left' came to the fore. When 'left' got a bad name, 'liberal' became the brand name, as it happened in the United States. In the US, the socialists have usurped the concept of 'liberal', so that 'a liberal' is now the opposite of its true meaning as being in favor of liberty. By these conceptual confusions, the socialists try to conceal the fact that socialism has been and always will be an inhuman system.

Antony P. Mueller

SYSTEMIC MISERY

Besides eliminating the rest of their opponents, redistribution marks the socialist seizure of power. Expulsion and liquidation go hand in hand.

Without economic growth, redistribution becomes pure capital consumption, and the shrinking capital stock makes the people poor. Income depends on production. And more income requires economic growth. One cannot distribute more than gets produced. If there is less production, there is less for consumption and less for investment. The income level depends on the capital stock and on the rate of innovation. If both decline, the wage rate must fall. Instead of a realm of plenty, socialism creates misery.

Paradoxically, the longing to realize the socialist dream comes in part from the great success of capitalism as an engine of prosperity. The modern entrepreneurial economy proves the enormous economic achievements that humanity can generate. The socialists believe that this great success would become even greater when one combines the productive capacity of capitalism with an equalitarian redistribution under the control of the state. This illusion was already evident in the Communist Manifesto of 1848, in which Karl Marx and his sponsor Friedrich Engels formulated their enthusiastic praise of the capitalist achievements of the so-called bourgeoisie.

In the same pamphlet, there is also a programmatic list of goals to transform capitalism into the socialist ideal.

Among the ten points, some party planks show how far socialism has already engulfed the economic systems of today:

- Strongly progressive taxes
- Centralization of credit in the hands of the state by a national bank with state capital and an exclusive monopoly
- Centralization of the transport system in the hands of the state
- Installation of national factories and production instruments, cultivation and improvement of the countryside according to a Community Plan
- Unification of the farmlands of agriculture and industry with the aim of gradually eliminating the contrast between town and country
- Public and paid education of all children, elimination of factory work of children in its present form, union of education with material production.

According to this Communist Decalogue, the items left to achieve full socialism are

- Requirement 1 - Expropriation of the landed property and use of the basic rent for state expenditure
- Requirement 4 - Confiscation of the property of all emigrants and rebels
- Requirement 8 - Equal obligation to work for all, establishment of an industrial army including in agriculture

If one compares these demands of the Communist Manifesto with the theses of the Party Program of the Nazis, whose official name was NSDAP, which means 'National Socialist German Workers Party', the similarity of the two catalogs show up regarding the individual demands and the spirit from which they are derived. In the NSDAP program of 1920, personally drawn up by Adolf Hitler, there are demands such as:

- Socialization of monopoly companies
- Municipalization of large department stores
- Expropriation of land for charitable purposes
- Prevention of real estate speculation
- Expansion of the entire education system
- Comprehensive system of scholarship stipends

along with goals as to health, fitness and a clean environment.

This selection of planks from both catalogs shows how similar the two lines of thought are. The two lists also show how far the claims of both ideologies have become a modern reality. It comes as no surprise that both the communist and the national-socialist governments have acted as repressive regimes that brought neither prosperity nor equality nor peace.

Socialism – whatever its kind - cannot exist without violence. If prices as an information and incentive system no longer exist, a command system must replace it. The socialist project leads to a command economy. The image of the 'new man' propagated by the socialists who contributes to production without self-interest or of the Aryan superman of the Nazis, turn out to be the opposite. In practice, socialism works by fear. When the Soviet Union was no longer able to exert terror, the regime collapsed. If the Hitler regime had not ended through war, it would have collapsed from its inner contradictions.

Under capitalism, in contrast, the economic actors adjust their behavior following their own interests in the face of scarcity because prices represent costs for the buyer and income and profits for the seller. The same applies to the entrepreneurial profit. In the capitalist economy, profits serve as an incentive and as an indicator of the extent to which the firm does the right thing according to the consumer's wishes. Losses signal inefficient production and coerce the company change its ways or leave the marketplace and thus make room for the more productive firms, which produce goods in a better way.

SUMMARY

The socialist utopia still attracts many people - despite the catastrophic outcomes that happened in all places where socialist systems took hold. Wherever there was socialism, there was also mass murder, oppression, and massacres. Social utopias are attractive. They satisfy the human wish for a paradise. Socialism shares with the other social utopias that the more one wants to realize the paradise on earth with the use of force the more one will create a hell. Not only did socialism fail to deliver the cherished expectations - the tragedy is that the reality of socialism has surpassed the worst expectations. It is the discrepancy between claim and reality that frightens and how much this system of horror was desired by many people and still is an ideal for some in our days.

The rulers need coercion so that everyone will follow the central plans. Under a socialist system, one cannot avoid becoming a law-transgressor because one cannot not survive without breaking the laws. In practice, socialism installs a power center, the Communist Party, which cooperates with the central economic planning apparatus, the secret police, and the military to suppress any dissent and to make sure that the voice of the people keeps silent and that the companies fulfill the plans.

Without market prices, following plans is always precarious because nobody knows how to fulfill the plan. Liquidation and deportation thus become a vital part a socialist rule. If everyone must break the laws and commands because it is impossible to follow them, there is also a secret list about each citizen, which compiles a person's inevitable trespassing and 'crimes'. Thereby, under socialism, everybody is a suspect and a criminal, first on paper, and, if need be, in front of the tribunal. In order to declare someone as guilty, the courts do not have to resort to prove the dissidence of the accused as the real cause of his prosecution, but it suffices to condemn the defendant because of an economic delinquency. Therefore, everyone in socialism is always at risk of persecution and incarceration. No one can feel safe since no one can remain innocent under such a regime.

When profit and loss no longer play a role, economic actors lose the orientation about what and how to produce. Even if socialism could have created this 'new man', and the ideal socialist man had emerged, he could not act economically, even if he wanted it to do, for lack of a price system to guide the allocation of resources. In socialism, there is an automatic tendency towards misallocation, waste, and inefficiency. 'Social prices' disregard scarcity. If the price of bread is made cheap, and at the same time there is no meat in the shops, consumers feed the cheap bread to pigs and chickens in their homes.

Even if one assumes that under socialism only good and educated persons would populate the country, socialism would fail nevertheless because the structure of the system does not provide the conditions to act rationally in the economy.

II.
THE FIASCO OF INTERVENTIONISM

"A government founded on the principle of benevolence to the people as a father to his children... is the greatest conceivable despotism .... The Sovereign will make the people happy according to his concepts and become despotism; the people will not let the universal human claim of their own happiness be taken and become a rebel."

Immanuel Kant: On the common saying: That may be correct in theory, but is not suitable for practice (1793)

- *Fascist roots of interventionism* -
- *Origins of modern state capitalism* –

- *Rational irrationality* –
- *Legacy of interventionism* –
- *Backgrounder: Effects of price interventionism* –
- *Interventionism and the market process* –
- *Employment* –
- *Power and economic law* –
- *Welfare: more costs than benefits* –
- *Healthcare costs* –
- *Cost explosion in education* –
- *Social policy* –
- *Backgrounder: origins of social policy* –
- *Missing standards* –
- *The chimera of social justice* –
- *Backgrounder: concepts of justice* –
- *Perpetual financial crisis* –
- *Backgrounder: the economics of the public debt* –
- *Backgrounder: where does the money comes from?* –
- *Capital, savings, and entrepreneurship* –
- *Summary*

The belief in interventionism has become so deep it resembles a religion. State activity is the new salvation without God. With the help from the state, the interventionist seeks to relief society from all ailments. The state has become the ultimate '*Deus ex machina*'. Yet the evils that the interventionist wants to cure through government intervention were often caused by the state itself. This way, interventionism does not solve problems but creates new troubles.

Interventionism is the so-called Third Way, an economic system between capitalism and socialism. This economic regime comes along with political populism and results in state capitalism and the growth of government. People like to praise this mixed system as a welfare state, but they fail to recognize that this kind of governance does not lead to the hoped-for Eldorado but is the path to stagnation.

Interventionism means a state-controlled economy and produces a perverse form of capitalism. Government intervention weakens the economic performance. The intervention in the market economy by the state leads first to disorientation among the economic agents, then to allocative distortions, and ends in a prolonged process when the economic activity slows down until it stagnates at a low level.

When the system has become fragile, it seems as if a failure of capitalism had occurred. The interventionists then conclude that new and even more comprehensive state intervention would be necessary to save the economy. Therefore, interventionism knows no end. It will always go on because intervention itself brings about the evils, which the government claims to remove.

The welfare state produces most of the social ailments, which the government claims to heal. The more generous the social assistance, the larger the number of social welfare recipients, the higher the burden of the social tax contributions, and the more the shadow economy will flourish. More complicated the tax code, more tax evasion takes place. The more access to public healthcare and medication, the sicker people become. The higher the percentage of a populational cohort that attends high schools and colleges, the lower the educational level.

RATIONAL IRRATIONALITY

Interventionism suffers from the conceit of knowledge. In his Nobel Prize speech of 1974, Friedrich Hayek diagnoses that the state planners overestimate their cognitive ability. They ignore that the more diverse the economy and society become, the more the economic coordination depends on a spontaneous order. The more complex the economy, the more important and indispensable are the markets.

The knowledge relevant to economic decision-making does not exist in a systematized form and is not available as a concentrated, organized set, but is tacit, fleeting, specific, and dispersed. Economic market knowledge relates to the specificity of place, time and people.

The division of labor in the market economy goes together with the division of knowledge in price-driven competitive markets.

The state intervention in economic life takes place without sufficient knowledge of the relevant circumstances. The motive of government intervention is not to resolve concrete problems, but to address political concerns. Without the explicit interest of specific groups, governmental action will not come into play.

Politics is not about solving problems; it is about to respond to special interests that brings forth specific concerns. The articulation of issues by the various groups is one-sided and influenced by the respective interests. Reliable statistics and detailed knowledge of facts about public issues are not available. Official statistics take a long time from the original collection data and their statistical treatment to their publication. Until the statistics reach the decision-makers, the actual situation has already changed.

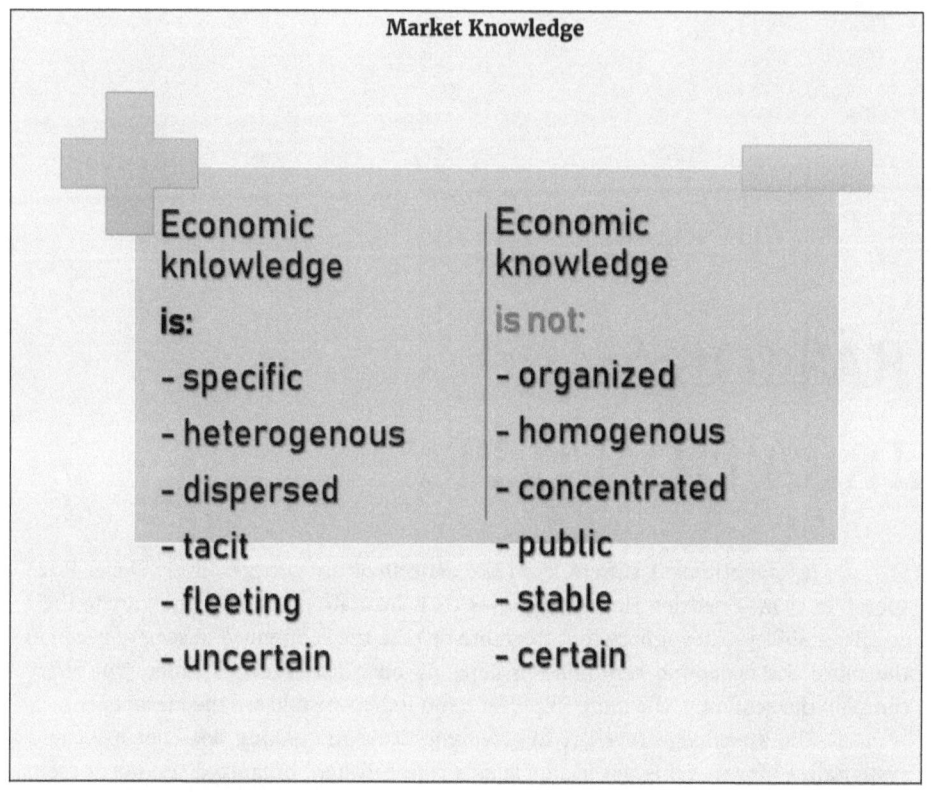

All statistics are history. Until the economic data reveal a clear picture and before the most relevant facts are gathered, the situation has changed again, and the social concerns have become different. Even if one could solve the information problem, the next barrier is how to reach a proper diagnosis and decide. The political process exists in a struggle to bundle, equalize or displace the diverse interests. The political decision-making is never about the issue itself. Politics is about interests and the representatives of certain interests are the issue.

By way of biased public discussion of socio-economic problems, even absurd political decisions receive popular support. The public debate is about values, which reflect interests. The representatives of special interest present their issue as a priority and as an absolute value. They do not consider that resources are limited in the face of the variety and of the plentitude of other needs and wishes. At the level of an individual, a family or a company, scarcity compels the decision-maker to weigh among the desires and to bring them into a ranking order so that the limited funds find an optimal use. Yet when public agencies decide, limited resources find no concern. Instead, specific interests dominate the discourse as these push their aims as unique absolute values. This happens because, in politics, not the same group which represents the specific interest bears the costs of a project but the collective of the taxpayers.

Even if a proper consensus about the diagnosis of the problem were available, it does not follow that politicians would use the appropriate means to solve the problem. Means are not neutral. Their use raises different costs, and the question is always to ask who will bear the costs associated with the project. Individual interests distort not only the political diagnoses and the objectives but also the use of the means.

In the political struggle, the loss in the fight for an issue of a relevant power group requires compensation. Concessions to one group raise demands from some other group. The wider the state distributes benefits the more other groups will emerge to claim their share. Consequently, there is no end to spending until the government runs out of money. When the game is over, everyone has been deceived and everyone feels betrayed. Therefore, the lobby never rests, and one negotiation session is only the prelude to the next. The more redistribution takes place, the more the people regard the system as unjust.

Interventionism suffers also from the problem that a considerable time elapses between information and diagnosis, and between the decision on the use of the means and the effect. Most times, the time span exceeds the regular legislative period. The government will not take sensible measures if the means bring costs now and only benefits later as it would be the case when the government reduces expenditures. In contrast, those measures receive priority that will offer present benefits and attract electoral votes now even when later the costs will exceed the benefits.

The monetarist economist Milton Friedman supported his doubts of a rational monetary policy by arguing that discretionary policies suffer from the lags of observation, decision, and effect. Yet not only monetary policy, but all types of public policies suffer from lags.

The decisions of governments take a long time to be made and a long time to take effect with the result that the pollical issue to be addressed has already fundamentally changed when the means begin to take effect. The problem runs even deeper than Friedman envisioned when one applies an individualist approach. All economic phenomena exist in human action. Thus, to gain complete picture the analysis must take human action into account. The lag problem is much wider and deeper when one considers that the political issues begins with individual expectation and the policy measures feedback on the expectations before they can become effective.

he popular view holds the present government responsible for what happens now - even if the current prosperity results from past actions or if the present gaiety of public spending will cause future misery. Under the system of party democracy, sensible decisions get through the political decision process only if they bring short-term benefits. Other measures must wait in the pipeline – often forever. Interventionism is populism. Interventionism hinders rational economic conduct. Therefore, interventionism, like socialism, does not represent a rational economic order.

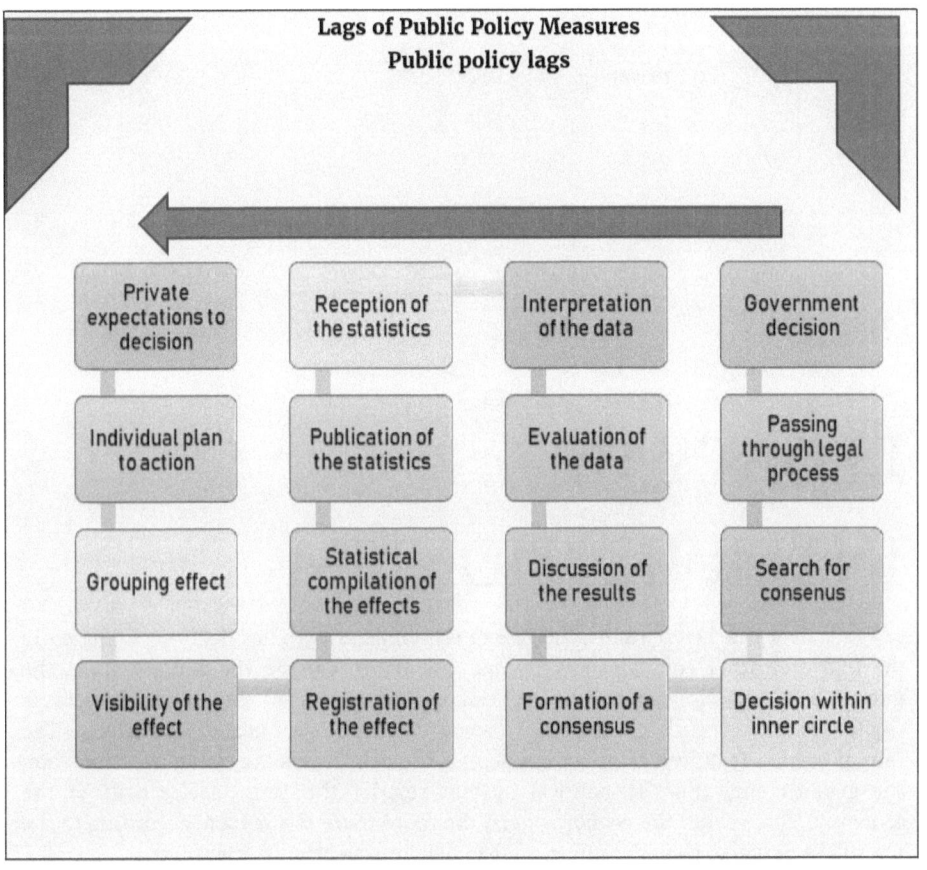

Antony P. Mueller

LEGACY OF INTERVENTIONISM

Over the past decades, the rate of economic growth has decreased. The more the USA and other countries maintained and try to expand the welfare state, the more the economic momentum subsided. The victim of the welfare state is capitalism and as much as capitalism was curtailed, the population has suffered. The rate of economic output is going down, and the debt levels are going up. The state, the government, and the political system restrict the free development of the economy. The weaker the economy gets, the more there is a reason, according to the prevailing perverse considerations, to take new interventionist measures.

A planned economy cannot cope with multiple aims the same way as the market economy can. This is also the case with interventionism, albeit here there are no fixed goals. Socialism is planned chaos. Interventionism is a chaotic planning.

The interventionist spiral takes hold of the economic policy as hyper-activism. If the economy does not recover with one interest rate cut, then the interest rate must fall further. When one government-spending program fizzles, a new one must follow. The more interventionism increases, the more capitalism gets the blame, even though the capitalist order is the victim of the interventionism. With all this political activism, one forgets that the cure for a weak economic performance is not more intervention but less government activity. Not more interventionism is the solution but more capitalism.

In the United States, the annual growth rate of the economy fell from around five percent in the 1950s and 1960s, to an annual rate of around two percent since 2000.

The publicized official growth rates would be smaller if the statistical bureaus of the governments would use the older methods of calculating the real GDP rate.

In as much as the official rate of inflation becomes lower, real gross domestic product and productivity will become statistically higher.

In Germany, the rate of economic growth of the gross domestic product fell from 8.2% in the 1950s to 1.6% in the 1990s and to 0.9% in the period 2000 to 2010. In Japan, the annual economic growth averaged 10 % from 1955 to 1970, around 5 % in the 1970s and 1980s, and has been in a slump ever since.

***

Interventionism hampers the dynamics of the markets and falsifies the price system. The administrative state perverts the market economy and reduces the effectiveness of the market as a coordination mechanism. The economic system gets weaker. Interventionism discourages innovation and leads to a waste of resources due to the cost of regulation and the misallocation brought about by the state intervention. The modern welfare-warfare state absorbs about half of the overall national production.

The central bank controls the money supply and the interest rate. All economic transactions are under bureaucratic authority. To speak of a 'savage capitalism' is evidence of grave ignorance and of ideological blindness. Capitalism in its present form is not a free capitalism. There is no predatory capitalism but a predatory state. While markets fail occasionally, governments fail systematically.

While socialism brings misery, distress, suppression of freedom, and a broken economy, this obvious failure of socialism does not quench the craving of the anti-capitalists to condemn the market economy. The critics denounce capitalism because it does not bring a paradise and because markets are not 'perfect' according to their imagination. The desire for the impossible is the reason for the popularity of the 'Third Way'. It promises a system beyond capitalism and socialism with the claim the best of the two worlds would merge. Yet there is no such thing as a perfect economic system where scarcity would disappear and social justice for all would find a home. The pretensions of the progressive movement that is behind the 'third way' is that there is an elite who has a special insight into what is right to improve the world. In their view, it is the government through which this progress will come about. In practice, however, the 'third way' makes capitalism less efficient. Progressivism is one more variant of the many socialist delusions.

The interventionists unite with special interest groups, who cloak their specific concerns as a common good. Under interventionism, the market competition perverts into a competition about subsidies and bailouts. The winners are no longer those who best contribute to the growth of the economy and serve the consumers, but those receive the largest share who have the best political contacts. In the end, no one is better off. In the long run, everyone is paying the price when the economy falters, including those who got a big share from the government when the economy was still flourishing.

In contrast to socialism, the interventions of the third way do not take place according to a central plan but happen ad hoc following populist-political criteria. Interventionism comprises a special order, which relates to the use of private property. A rental control, for example, leaves the private property formally intact but restricts the scope of pricing. The 'third way' leads to the fiscal state, to the gradual erosion of private property, and to the creeping confiscation of private income and wealth.

While there is little controversy about the harmfulness and economic inefficiencies of direct price interventions, the government bureaucrats ignore the effects of indirect interventions. Most economists know how price interventions, as it is the case in agriculture, for example, lead to misallocation. Yet there are few who likewise condemn the interventionism that comes with welfare policy, labor market regulation, environmental policy, pension and health policy, education, taxation, financial market regulation, and monetary policy. Nevertheless, a look at these areas of intervention reveals that these are the same areas where the misallocation of recourses is the greatest and the dissatisfaction of the population is most widespread. The interventionist policies are to solve problems when in fact more new problems emerge as the result of interventionism than old problems get solved.

The great illusion of our time is the expectation that special state interventions can settle our problems. But there are no perfect solutions available, to begin with. Public problems have no solutions, only trade-offs. Here is the poodle's core: the state is notoriously unable to evaluate the available options and weigh benefits against costs. The government either makes no trade-off at all or, when it does, comes to the wrong results because of one-sidedness and public pressure. The members of the bureaucracy know very well that government activity lacks wisdom and if there is a reasonable decision, it comes more from accident than by design.

The state bureaucracy must replace evaluation and judgment by statistical indicators, reference numbers and the whole flood of quantitative controls and political criteria. Cases are not rare when grotesque misallocations occur. The assessment of medical doctors takes place in line with the number of their operations, and more patients get surgeries than necessary. The evaluation of science comes not from scientific content, but by the number and place of publications. Teachers receive their assessment according to the failure rate of their students and grade inflation sets in.

The problem with state interventionism is that it fails not only to solve the problems and that it creates new ones, but that state intervention systematically excludes private solutions. Interventionism makes society less open to opportunities for success. It reduces the innovative power and paralyzes the private initiative both directly through regulation and indirectly through the tax burden. Interventionism closes the space for innovations.

Any alleged solution entails specific costs. These costs are not just the immediate costs that are obvious but also the plethora of undetected consequential costs that are difficult to discover and impossible to quantify and to forecast. Since there are no definitive solutions, problems remain, and this is the reason there seems to be a constant need for renewed interventionist efforts. Each government intervention aims at a specific problem and promises its 'solution'. Yet with the growing number of interventions, a network of problematic constellations arises, so that with each new state intervention the problems do not decrease, but they multiply. Interventionism, in contrast to markets, cannot cope with complexity. In a modern economy, interventionism must fail.

Policy interventions produce confusion, disgust, and indolence among the population, yet people demand more, and politicians are keen to promise delivery. Popular talk denounces the politicians, but hardly anyone names evil by its name: interventionism. There is no one who could have all the knowledge about the intricacies of the tax code or of the social legislation. If the government adopts a new measure, no official, secretary, or minister can state what would be its effects. The scientific reports of alleged governmental advisors are worthless. First, because experts also do not have complete information, and second because if they should expose deviating opinions, they would diminish their chances of being hired for the next project. The larger an institution, be it a private company or a state, the higher the transaction costs and the less the transparency. Companies know there are not only advantages of size but also costs of size and limit the expansion of their production units. If a company grows beyond its optimal size, profits fall. Yet with no system of profit and loss in the public sector, there is no warning signal of misallocation with interventionist policies.

Effects of Price Interventionism

Free market

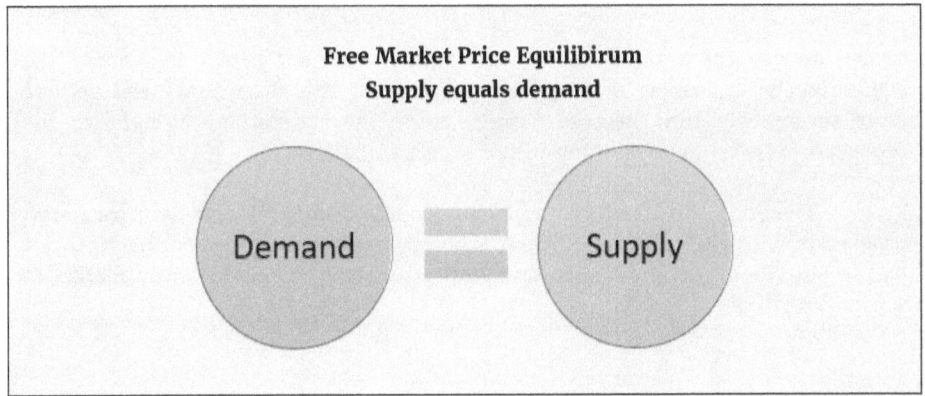

Interventions change the market outcome and produce distortions. When government installs a price ceiling, prices are kept low. Instead of doing away with the shortage, this policy leads to a contraction of supply and an increase in demand. Because producers do not receive the market price, there will also be less investment to produce this good. Therefore, price ceilings produce not only a temporary shortage but perpetuate the market disequilibrium.

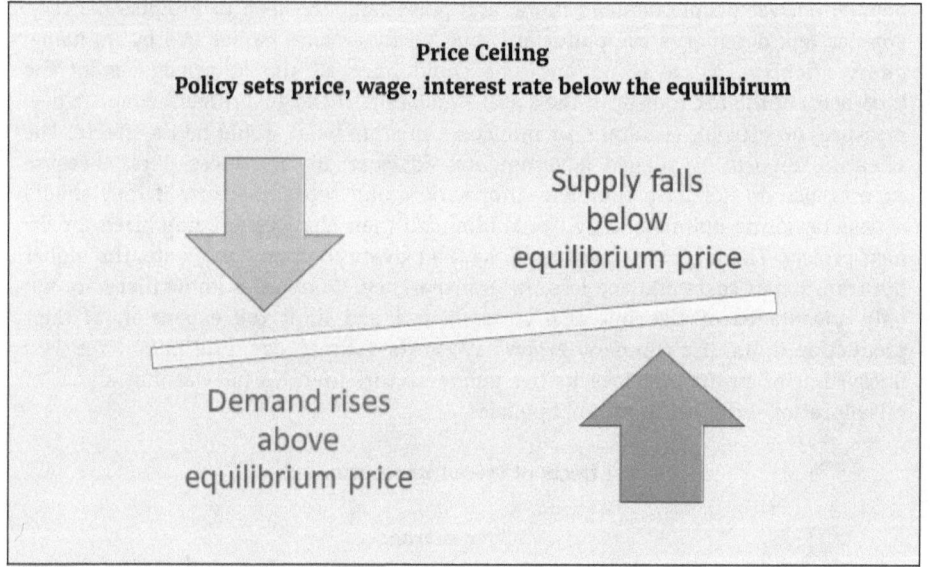

In the case of a price floor, when the government sets prices above the equilibrium price, supply rises while demand falls. This discrepancy will become more severe over time because a price above the equilibrium incentivizes the producers to invest more and thus future supply will increase.

The European Union has applied price floors in many areas of agricultural production with the result of a massive overproduction. The responsible agencies had to buy the excess production and store it or dump it on the world market at subsidized prices.

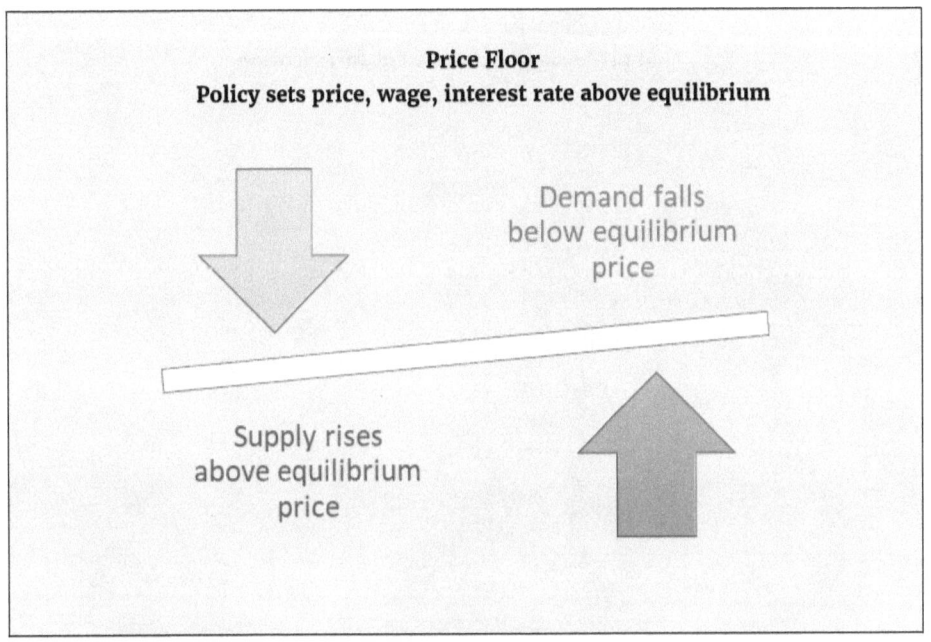

In addition to the market interventions, the state's activities include monetary affairs and interventions in property rights.

Market interventions refer to price and quantity controls as well as to competition policy. The Constitution protects private property only to a limited extent. Money is under direct state control. Issuing of circulating money in the form of notes is the responsibility of the central bank which also has powers to control the distribution of money by the private commercial banks.

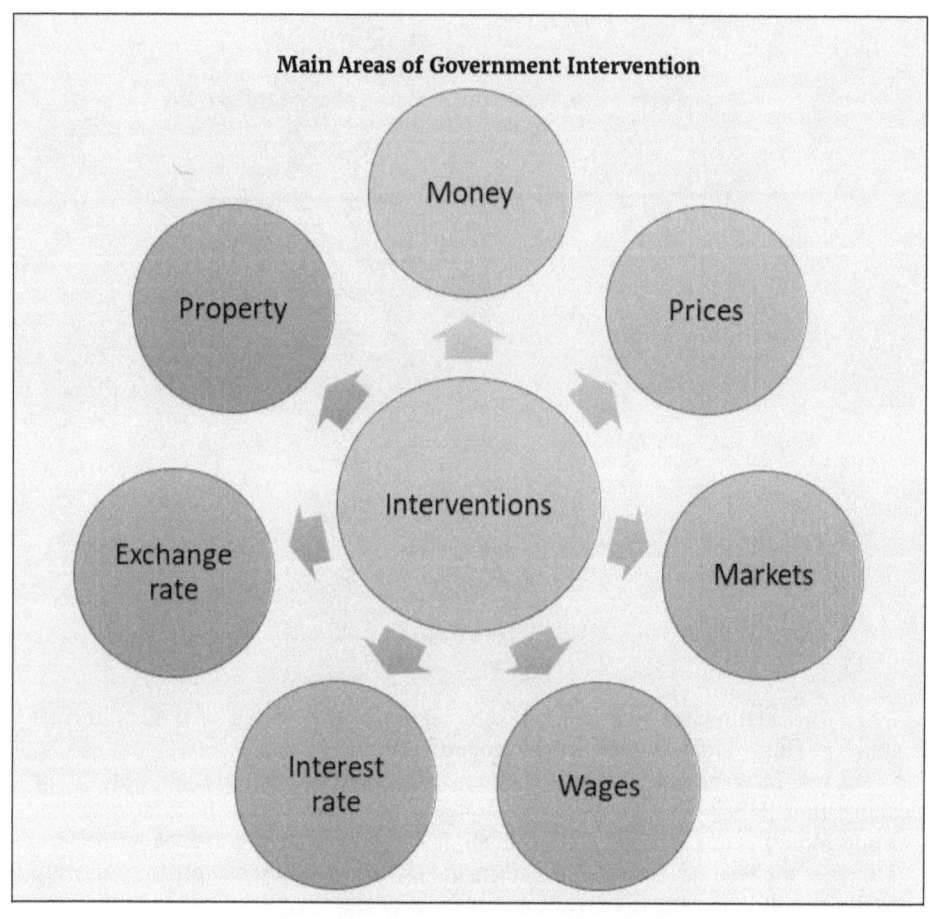

INTERVENTIONISM AND THE MARKET PROCESS

Among the three basic ways of coping with the uncertainty of the future -- gambling, speculation, and engineering -- speculation is the way of human action when dealing with economic and financial matters. Speculation is the basic mode of entrepreneurial judgment. Even more so, speculation is how human action deals with the future.

Speculation as the entrepreneurial judgment would be unnecessary if the future were not uncertain. Then it would be possible to calculate the future structure of the market and economics could become a reliable forecasting profession. Yet "the entrepreneurial idea that carries on and brings profit is precisely that idea which did not occur to the majority. It is not correct foresight as such that yields profits, but foresight better than that of the rest. The prize goes only to those dissenters who do not let them be misled by the errors accepted by the multitude. What makes profits emerge is the provision for future needs for which others have neglected to make adequate provision." (Ludwig von Mises in Human Action, p. 867)

In this view, it is futile to base economic decisions on formulas. Human action must use relative prices as the guideposts for making plans, but information and the numbers which appear as prices do not speak for themselves and instead one must assess, compare and relate them to one's personal value system. The same original bit of information has various shades of meaning for different persons and often it is of a very different quality as to its practical relevance. Prices cannot substitute judgment. They are tools to make judgments.

The market process exists in action and reaction of extreme complexity even at the level of simple goods. The market process coordinates the diverse subjective valuations of the immense variety of individual plans all of which are not observable beyond the prices. The structure of relative prices does not reflect agreement on valuations, but the observable exchange ratios in the market are the product of a discrepancy in attributing values. Prices, although they convey information, do not imply that these are correct or efficient. Prices coordinate, they neither measure nor evaluate.

What is available to the observer as 'present prices' are in fact past prices as they reflect the conditions of the past. Past prices do not determine future prices - but to anticipate future prices determine the current prices. Expected prices are also those prices, which are relevant to price complementary goods and to remunerate the factors of production. What counts for the entrepreneurial judgment are neither past nor present prices, but the expected prices.

Without entrepreneurial judgment that deals with expected prices instead of current prices, as bureaucrats must, there is no way to cope with the vicissitudes of a dynamic economy. Present prices suffice to allocate the resources in a stagnant economy; they do not coordinate economic activities in a growing economy.

Equilibrium in terms of fulfillment of expectations is temporary. Market prices are volatile because they reflect the uncertainty of our expectations, which is even more pronounced when evaluating the value of assets. Governments that presume that due to their position of authority they could do away with this instability, base their cause on the belief that bureaucracies are better equipped to deal with the uncertainties of the future than the individual entrepreneurs and the individual consumers. By doing so, they disregard the essence of markets.

Market interventions mislead the adaptation process of individual actors. They add further elements of uncertainty to the formation of expectations and frustrate the expected courses of action. The popularity of interventionism -- defined as the efforts of political authorities to reallocate resources other than in a free market -- can be explained in terms of political interests. Epistemologically, however, interventionism stands on very weak grounds once the assumption of determinism gets discarded.

Not less so than the direct interventions in individual product markets, macroeconomic intervention and the stabilization of the price level disrupt the coordination process. Macroeconomic aggregates are ill-defined concepts and of dubious statistical validity. The conceptual units that are used in macroeconomic policy are statistical constructs and their presumed causal connection lacks reliability. Statistical averages neither act nor can they cause a phenomenon.

The stabilizers and interventionists ignore that error is essential to human action. They postulate failures of the market yet for themselves they claim to be free of the errors. The stabilizers ignore their own fallibility and negate that in a world where the future is unknown, the occurrence of errors -- or disequilibria when defined in terms of the fulfillment of expectations -- is a necessary part of the human action in a complex and dynamic environment with numerous interactions. Unhampered markets receive their privileged status in this context, not from the chimera of being perfect but because they allow continuous adaptation, i.e. the constant correction of misallocations as they are identified by subjective valuations. All models of the so-called market failure suffer from the deficiency that they take the perceived errors for permanent and ignore that what matters is not that errors occur, which is unavoidable, but that the market as a process works to correct the errors.

In a market economy, there is no such thing as certainty about the future prices. The status of wealth, which is attributed to a certain arrangement of capital goods by the market process, is always at stake. It is this insight into the changing nature of wealth that differentiates the Austrian approach from the preachers of stabilization. Likewise, the idea of social justice has no place in a capitalist economy. The problems with just or unjust distribution pertain to pre-capitalist societies with quasi-stationary economies where the ownership of resources -- predominantly land and serfs -- implies the automatic access to a yield. Under capitalist conditions, however, there is a need for an on-going re-pricing of capital goods with the consequence of a permanent process of redistribution.

We live in a world of unexpected change. "The maintenance of wealth is always problematical; and in the long run it may be said to be impossible." (Ludwig Lachmann)

The market process is the great leveler. By coordinating demand and supply, the market process also redistributes wealth.

In socialism, the ultimate rationale for state control is the deceitful promise of social justice. A similar kind of pretense continues to form the basis of the apparent legitimacy for government interventions when it comes to the stability of the economy or to social security and equal redistribution. In the light of these concepts, a market economy always must appear as deficient. By applying the ideas of stability and social justice as policy guides, each failed interventionist policy measure will only provide one more reason for additional measures. In the light of the theory of the market process, the dramatic failure of socialism comes as no surprise. Likewise, the fixation of modern governments with stability, social security, and redistribution must fail; and the more these goals are being pursued the more likely these policies will end in a collapse.

EMPLOYMENT

The declaration of a 'right to work' is without a rational foundation as it disregards who will provide the capital that enables employment. The problem is not 'work' but having a workplace. To look for a job is, in fact, the search for a place to work, and the search for a workplace is the search for capital. If there were no need for capital, then the unemployed could work right away as self-employed. Unemployment means that there is a lack of capital in this economy.

The stock of capital determines the potential of employment and the level of productivity. Unemployment occurs when the productivity of the worker is too low compared to the wage rate. The wage rate must fall, or productivity must increase to do away with unemployment. Therefore, as the classical economics pointed out, only voluntary unemployment happens in a market economy. Unemployment means that wage claims are too high compared to labor productivity. The productivity of labor, in turn, is too low when the economy does not have sufficient capital and lacks technological progress. Rising wages and more jobs require capital formation. It is only with the corresponding capital stock that the labor force becomes productive. Unemployment disappears when the wage rates adjust to productivity. To do away with unemployment, either wage rates must fall, or productivity must rise.

If workers raise wage rates through trade union power that exceed productivity, unemployment occurs because companies must reduce their workforce. Power, including trade union power, cannot break the fundamental economic laws. As with other markets, in the labor market, too, price interventions lead to quantitative reactions. If the price of labor is too high, the result is the dismissals of workers and a decline in the number of jobs offered by the companies.

It is a common error to believe the use of machines in production would lead to unemployment when in fact capital accumulation makes it possible that workers move from less productive jobs into those with higher productivity where they can earn higher salaries. The increase in wages results from more capital and from technical progress in these advanced sectors of the economy. Not trade unions and government intervention lift wages, but capital accumulation and technological progress.

In the 1930s, the link between wage level and employment, which classical economics had well elaborated, came under fire by the doctrine of the English economist John Maynard Keynes (1883-1946). According to Lord Keynes, employment depends on aggregate demand. For Keynes, the cause of unemployment is not the shortage of capital but the insufficient overall demand. The Keynesian recipe of bringing down unemployment is to increase spending by the state financed by an increase of the government debt. This school claims that the expenditure program would pay for itself because spending creates income, and incomes serve to stimulate the demand. The plain fact that public debt has been rising since the 1970s indicates the failure of Keynesian doctrine. The legacy of Keynes is not full employment and economic growth but inflation and stagnation.

Types of unemployment

Like with the 'wage mismatch', it is questionable to categorize 'skills mismatch' as involuntary unemployment. After all, the workmen are obliged to gain marketable skills.

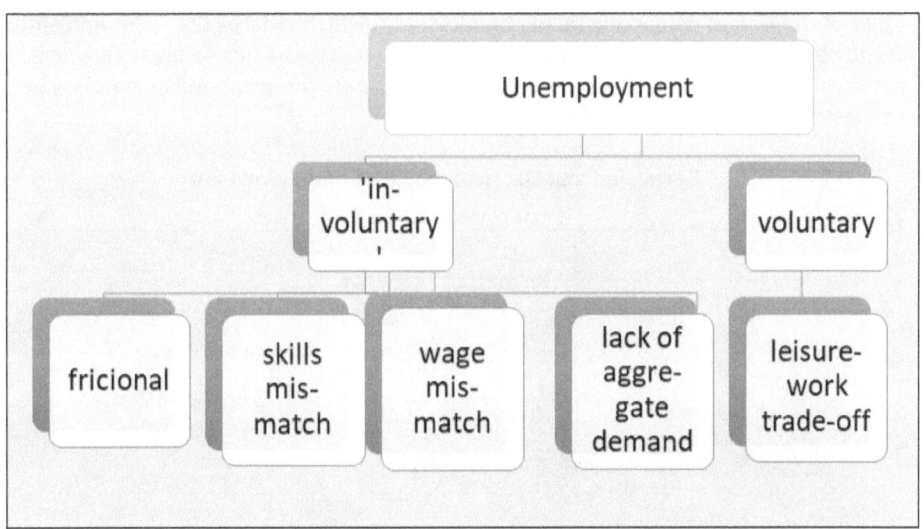

Skills mismatch, like frictional unemployment, is not necessarily 'involuntary' because it happens as the effect of the structural changes that come with a dynamic economy. As such, they are a normal ingredient of a market economy. Skills mismatch is comparable to falling sales and profits of a company that has an obsolete product line and will go out of business when it does not adapt to the new market conditions. Keynes' theory of involuntary unemployment postulates that persistently high unemployment is neither lack of capital nor of a wage mismatch but results from a lack of aggregate demand. If this theory were correct, one could do away with unemployment as fast as the government would spend more.

**

The Keynesian theory of aggregate demand ignores scarcity and costs. While it is true that the income, which some person spends, is income received by someone else, it is also true that wages – while income for the worker – are costs for the employer. In the Keynesian perspective, wages can never be too high because they represent income and thus spending. Yet if labor costs are higher than the contribution of labor to production, it does not matter whether there is more demand or less demand because losses result when labor costs exceed the contribution of labor to production. Business cannot survive without profit, whatever the demand.

The relationship between aggregate demand and employment runs in the opposite direction as postulated in the Keynesian model. Wage rates that are too high in terms of productivity lead to unemployment, and unemployment leads to a fall in demand. As the classical economic theory states, not lack of demand causes unemployment, but wage rates that exceed productivity lead to layoffs. The true cause of the lack of demand is falling employment, which reduces the wage sum and diminishes aggregate demand. Not the economic weakness leads to unemployment, but the unemployment - caused by high wages - causes the economic weakness. The Keynesians mistake the effect for the cause.

Keynesian and classical model of unemployment

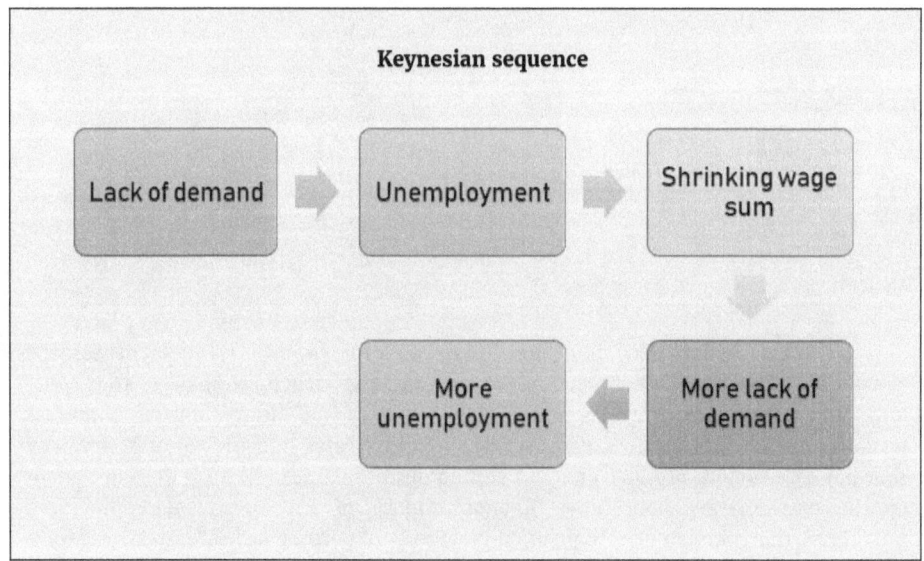

The Keynesian theory postulates without further ado a 'lack of demand', which causes unemployment and leads to a downward spiral where lack of demand increases unemployment, and the unemployment reduces demand.

The Keynesian solution is government intervention: the injection of extra demand through 'deficit spending'.

The classical model, in contrast, has a theory about the causes of unemployment and how a free labor market eliminates unemployment. According to the classical sequence, unemployment results when the wage rates exceed productivity and compels business to reduce employment. Rising unemployment, however, brings down the wage rate and thus leads a new equilibrium with no involuntary unemployment.

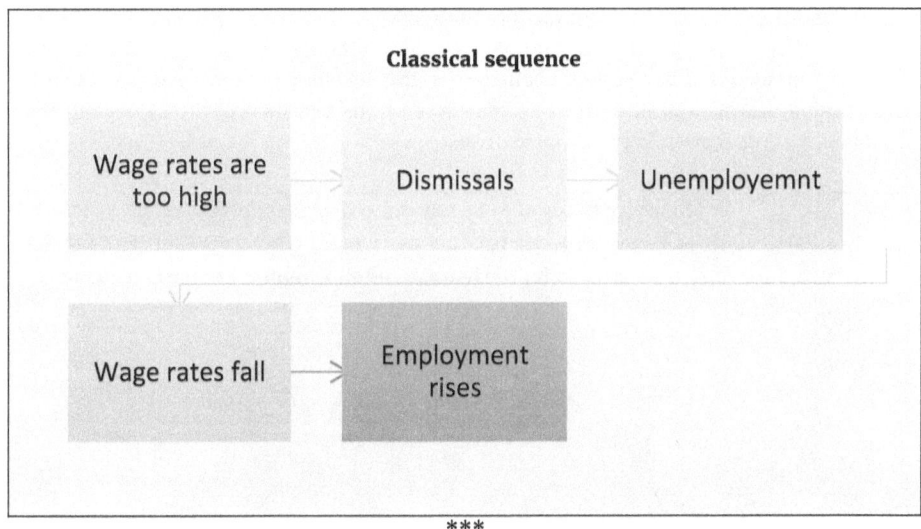

***

Not different from earlier times, contemporary doomsayers fear mass unemployment due to the automation of production by robots. They put forth the same arguments as was the case at the time of the industrial revolution. Then, the weavers and other craftsmen feared the loss of their workplace because of the steam engine as the result of more sophisticated production devices. However, it is a historical fact that the technological advances that accompanied the industrial revolution have created a multiplicity of jobs. While the new machines saved labor in agriculture, jobs expanded by the multiples in the new industries.

While over two-thirds of the workforce still worked in agriculture at the beginning of the 19th century, they now account for about two percent in the industrialized countries.

In as much as the new technologies eliminate jobs, including sophisticated positions, productivity counts to bring down the costs of living. A policy of keeping the jobs safe would be the wrong approach because it would hold the economy down on a low productivity level and thus keep people poor.

In a free economy, technological unemployment loses its threat. This warning ignores that the automation of the economy drives up productivity. High wage rates require a high technological standard. Productivity determines the wage level. Wages are higher in the industrialized countries because their productivity is higher than that of poor countries. Because of the high level of productivity, simple activities, too, receive a better remuneration. The high remuneration for ordinary jobs drives the people from the poor countries to migrate to the rich places. The Mexican agricultural worker in California multiplies his earnings in the United States doing the same work as at home because the general productivity in the US is higher than in Mexico. Excess labor is the scourge of the poor countries because they lack capital and therefore suffer from low productivity.

While the dearth of capital is the fundamental cause of persistent unemployment in the developing countries, in the developed market economies with their high stock of capital, there is no reason of enduring unemployment beyond the effects of wrong economic policy measures.

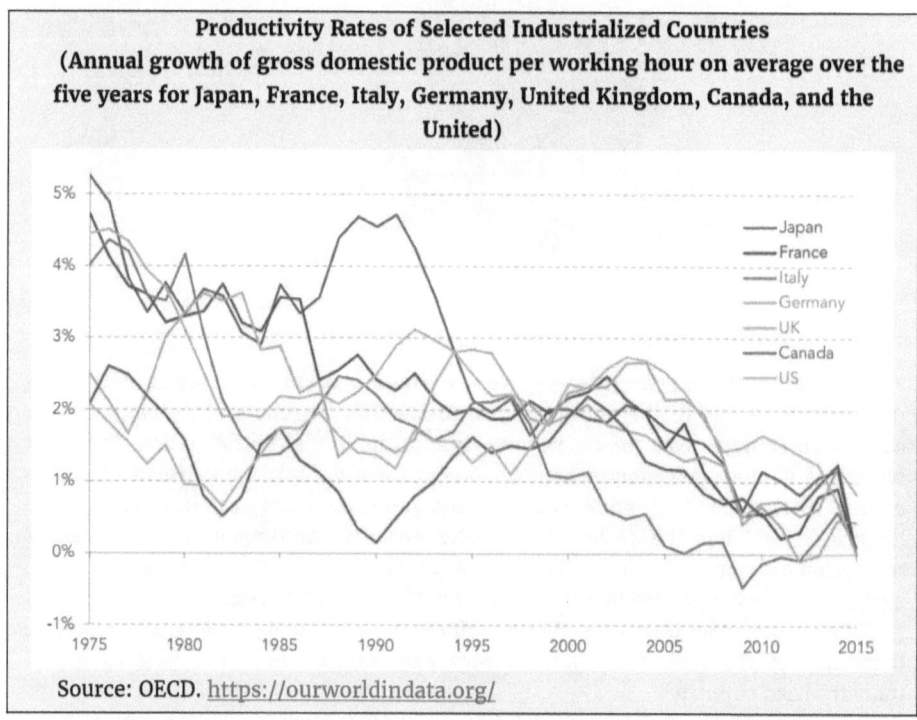

Since 1975, the rates of productivity gains have been sinking in the industrialized countries, and since about 2007, productivity growth in the advanced industrialized countries has been almost stagnating. This means that wage increases and working time reductions will be limited for the years to come. In such a situation, a politically motivated expansive spending policy would be poison for the national economy. The answer to this challenge is less state, less bureaucracy, and less government debt.

***

POWER AND ECONOMIC LAW

In the same way that government cannot eliminate the natural laws, state intervention cannot do away with the market laws. Under interventionism, the laws of economics maintain their validity, albeit in a distorted way. This rule applies to trade union power. A single union can raise the wage rate for its members but when all trade unions go on strike and achieve higher wage rates in tandem, no worker will be better off. On the contrary, if the wage rate increases at the expense profits, the pace of accumulation of capital falls. When the capital stock gets smaller, wage rates must fall, and less hiring will take place. The chain of causation goes from higher wage rate to less capital, and from less capital to lower productivity to unemployment and to lower wage rates.

Trade union power may push wage rates higher, yet when they exceed productivity, profits fall, and less capital accumulation will take place. Rising labor costs cause the demand for labor to fall and lay-offs to rise. Higher unemployment implies that aggregate labor income falls, and mass unemployment follows. Instead of improving the fate of the workers, the excessive demand for higher wages has achieved the opposite.

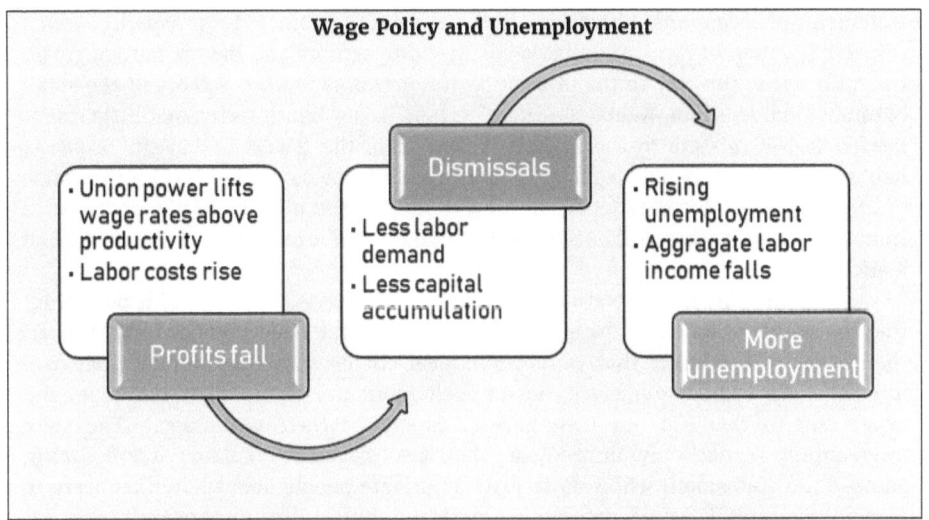

One can contrast the neoclassical answer and the Keynesian policy recipe in one sentence: Neoclassical economics says that wage rates should fall, while Keynesian economics says that aggregate demand should rise.

***

When government introduces price controls, the outcome of the law of supply and demand changes from price to quantity. If the legislative body abolishes the private property rights to eliminate supposed deficiencies, more scarcity results since the production incentives are lost. Despite this, authoritarian thinking prevails in the public sphere and the belief prevails that the laws of the state could overcome the laws of economics. Many people still think all it would take to make things better were the promulgating of more laws. Yet while a government can arbitrarily oblige the people to drive on the right side as opposed to the left, the state cannot oblige the water to flow upwards and violate gravity or to induce economic agents to act against the law of supply and demand.

The concept of the law, including that of natural laws and the market laws, comes originally from the sphere of legislation. Until the eighteenth century, the idea prevailed that man was subject to religion and authority, and ultimately to God. The same way as nature has its own laws, the economy and the society have their own principles.

In the Scottish Enlightenment of the 18th century and with Immanuel Kant (1724-1804), the new science of the economy and society showed that the economy and society have laws of their own. It was Adam Smith (1723-1790), who - with Adam Ferguson (1723-1816) and David Hume (1711-1776) – formulated such laws for the society. In his "Theory of Moral Sentiments" (1759) and for the economy in his work about "The Wealth of the Nations" (1776), Adam Smith elaborates the basic statement of economic liberalism that this nation comes to prosperity which respects the market laws, and that keeps the state activity and the tax burden small. In Smith' view, the way to the prosperity of a nation is not the activity of the state, but individual freedom. In his "Lectures" (1755), Adam Smith states that little else is needed to lead a state to the highest wealth from the lowest barbarism as peace, light taxes, and a tolerable legal system: everything else comes by the natural course of things. "Little else is requisite to carry a state to the highest degree of opulence from the lowest barbarism, but peace, easy taxes, and a tolerable administration of justice..."

In his "Wealth of Nations" (Book One, Chapter 2), Adam Smith points out that the supply of food and drink does not depend on the benevolence of the butcher, the brewer or the baker that we get our meal but because they pursue their own interest. "We address ourselves, not to their humanity but to their self-love, and never talk to them of our own necessities but of their advantage." The state intervention is not only unnecessary but also harmful, explains Adam Smith, because the statesman, who was to instruct private people about how they were to invest their capital, would not only be burdened with a very unnecessary task, but also would seize an authority, which is nowhere so dangerous as in the hands of a man who has enough folly and arrogance to feel capable of exercising that authority. (Book IV, Chapter 2).

In politics, however, it is common to ignore the laws of the economy. On the political battlefield, the guiding principle is that one could shape the economy and society at will – and be it by applying brute force. This conviction comes along with the positivist legal thinking, according to which law is what the legislator decides to be legal. This belief in the omnipotence of legislation and of the state dominates the expansion of the welfare state and promotes interventionism.

With the claim to arbitrary legislation, the legal positivists ignore the original idea of the law and violate the principle of the validity of law beyond the will of man. The modern lawgivers act as if they were gods and could declare at will anything they want as 'the law of the state'. Yet the basic idea of law is that it is not a creation but a discovery. In the traditional, pre-positivist legal theory, to be deemed legitimate, laws had to conform to the physical world and to the essence of the human nature. The principle says that man cannot and must not shape his environment to one's own predilections but that one must respect the laws of nature and of society. For economic and social policy, this means that the person who opposes the economic laws must pay the corresponding price. In this sense, the rule holds that when one chooses a system against the human nature, such as socialism, society will earn poverty and suppression. Equally, although at a different level, if the trade unions succeed to push up the wage rate above the equilibrium level which productivity sets, retribution in terms of unemployment sets in. When the state inflates the money supply to counteract unemployment, inflation is the result. A man is free in his choice, but not in the consequences of his choice.

III.

WELFARE: MORE COSTS THAN BENEFITS

For many people, the welfare state is a great achievement. Yet few people recognize that the more comprehensively the welfare state extends its realm, the more the beneficiaries themselves must bear the costs. The citizens pay for what they receive and, in addition to it, they pay also for the apparatus that has emerged around the distributive state in the form of administrative expenses and the rent-seeking by special interest groups. There is a welfare industry in existence that ranges from the medical-pharmaceutical complex to the employment opportunities of social workers.

The wealthy persons of the society will care for the poor if redistribution remains small and if the circle of the needy is well defined. This is the case with voluntary charity. Yet when the state expands into the welfare state, the beneficiaries of the social transfers must de facto assume the costs themselves for what they seem to get free from the state. The more the general population falls into the grip of the welfare state, the more diffuse the definition of need becomes and the larger the number of the contributors will grow. In the end, all pay more than they get.

At a deeper level, the evils that many citizens attribute to 'capitalism' are the result of the fact that these very same citizens demand from the political parties what they lament. As the French libertarian pamphleteer Frédéric Bastiat (1801-1850) observed, the state is that fiction where each one tries to live at the expense of all other people. The social state means that the services it provides become more expensive than they would be under private supply. For example, under a system of general health insurance, medical services cost more than they would cost in the free market if there were no state insurance schemes. Because an insurance exists, demand for its services rises, including for many superfluous purposes. Instead of utility-driven, the system becomes cost-driven. Prices continue to rise even when the benefits of the services sink. As the costs rise, the quality of the supply falls.

The term 'moral hazard' comes from the insurance industry. The concept designates the phenomenon that insurance produces incentives to provoke the damage that the insurance covers. The prices of the insured product and services will rise. The profiteers from insurance are those groups that provide the good, which the insurance covers. With the car insurance, it is auto repair shops and with health, it is the health providers, the medical doctors, and the pharmaceutical industry. For the healthcare system, moral hazard signifies that the great beneficiary of a comprehensive health insurance system is the medical establishment - such as hospitals, medical doctors, and the health industry, while the clients are the losers as they must bear the extra costs. An obligatory insurance is financially a magic boon to the suppliers of the goods and services for which there is an insurance. Likewise, the largest beneficiaries of the subsidies that students receive from the state to study are the employees of colleges, with their administrators at the top.

Since its inception, dissatisfaction with the welfare state has increased at the same tempo as the costs of the welfare state have risen. Since its beginning, social security was sold to the public as an offer that apparently would come costless. Since then, this illusion is also upheld as to the whole range of programs of the comprehensive welfare state. Consequently, the demand for all kinds of social policies systematically exceeds the supply, even if almost everyone is dissatisfied with the performance of the system.

HEALTHCARE COSTS

The more comprehensive the insurance coverage is, the higher are the additional costs caused by the moral hazard. The health care system has become so expensive because of the large number of insured persons who have easy access to full healthcare.

The existence of a state-run health insurance system drives up the costs for the private insurers and the private consumers as well. A rarely noticed effect of a widespread healthcare system is that it pushes up the costs for the private payer. The higher the number of the insured, the more increases the incentive of the uninsured to get an insurance, which makes the system even more inefficient.

Due to the demographic development and the further expansion of the medical-pharmaceutical complex, studies predict that health care contribution rates would rise to between 25% and 30% of the personal income in the coming decades when no system change will take place without much benefit in terms of longevity.

The chart below shows the price changes of medical care and college tuition compared to software and TVs from 1997 to 2017 based on the price index for average urban consumer prices.

Health care spending does not provide a significant increase in life expectancy if the expenditure is more than about two hundred US dollars per month.

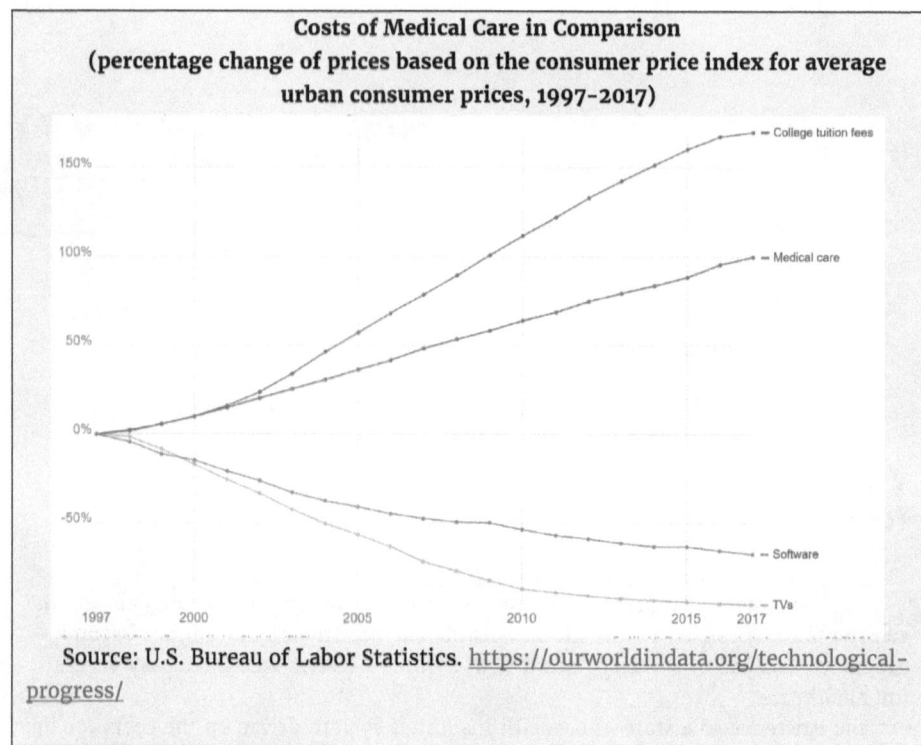

Source: U.S. Bureau of Labor Statistics. https://ourworldindata.org/technological-progress/

The curve indicates that the medical spending reaches is maximum positive effect at about two thousand dollars per year. Even this sum may be too high because spending on health up to $ 2,000 happens thanks to the benefits that come with the growth of the economy, so that part of the increase in life expectancy is not due to health spending, but rather to the growth-related increase of the overall quality of life (Max Roser https://ourworldindata.org/life-expectancy/).

The data of the United States support this thesis. Although the United States has the highest per capita spending on health, life expectancy is lower than in that of comparable countries. At present, the limit of the best general life expectancy is about 80 years. Expenditure on health spending of over 2,000 dollars a year does not increase this limit.

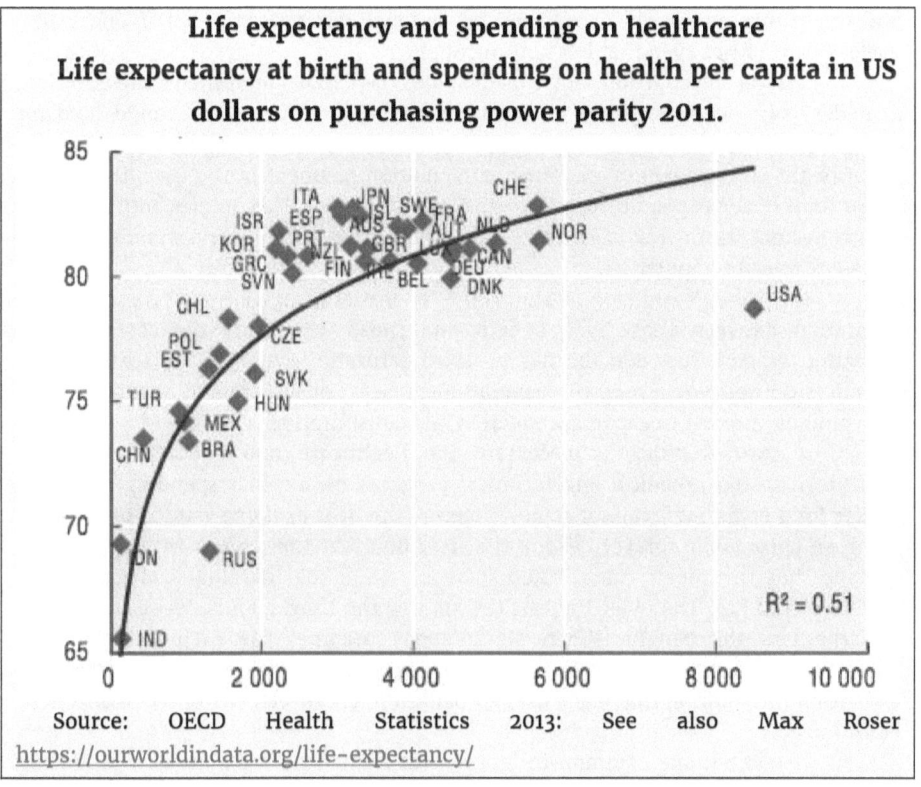

Source: OECD Health Statistics 2013: See also Max Roser
https://ourworldindata.org/life-expectancy/

***

Today, the healthcare system has become an institution where a massive redistribution takes place from the young people and the active workforce to the old and inactive part of the population. While the benefits of the care for the elderly are questionable and an ethical issue, the burden that falls on the active part of the population is obvious. Expenditure on healthcare is a deadly trend. Incurable patients absorb increasingly resources as expenditure flow into the diagnosis because no therapy works and because of the costs for the individual patient concentrate in the last few years or often just months of one's life with dubious benefits and immense costs.

It is difficult to answer the question for which activity more public spending is a waste: for health or for education. In any case, both areas suffer from the rise in costs, which exceed that of the rise of the cost of living in general. Both systems suffer from a fundamental deficiency of control because there is no direct linkage between the costs and the individual demand. Without personal cost bearing, the insured consult the doctor, even if it were unnecessary and may even be harmful, and the young attend the subsidized educational institutions, even if one learns useless stuff or not even that but nothing at all.

Taking the contribution of medicine to the extension of life as the criterion, a modest sum of expenditure on health would suffice. The same would hold for education. If these systems were private, costs would sink. However, since the benefits are independent of the direct contribution payment of the user, there is no upper limit of the expenditure, and costs continue to rise. This applies both to a state health system as to a system that makes insurance compulsory and that covers almost the entire population.

Like the healthcare system, the educational system suffers from the separation between those who benefit and those who carry the costs. In the education system, too, demand has no fixed saturation point. If the costs for the providers do not play a role, the demand increases. Consumers and suppliers share the common interest to expand production and consumption.

A new thinking is necessary for healthcare and education. For the healthcare system, medical and technical progress means that spending goes into efforts for a goal that it cannot achieve: eternal life. It is as if one wanted to continue using an automobile forever despite the wear and tear that comes with aging. It is obvious that the repair costs would increase while the marginal benefits of the repairs would fall. The older the car, the shorter the time span between the repairs and the less the benefit. When maintenance becomes the exclusive objective, technical progress brings rising costs with little benefit. Such systems set a cost expansion into motion that leads to their bankruptcy. One can wish it were different, but it is not.

It has become common to ignore that human nature aims at reproducing life and not only at life extension and its maintenance. If everyone were to bear the costs personally, demand would stop when marginal utility no longer exceeds marginal costs. This would also be the case for health services, since some questionable treatments, which would be technically possible, would no longer be in demand. With insurance, however, there is no resistance from the patient concerning the interest of the suppliers of health services to apply as many services as possible at prices - and therefore of costs - that are as high as possible.

An insurance scheme, when organized as a collective system as it is the case with health insurance, brings with it that the users will ignore the principle of marginal utility and marginal costs. The gates are thus open to a cost avalanche. If no change of the system will occur, the healthcare Moloch will absorb increasingly of the income of the population, until at the theoretical limit health costs would use up a person's entire income. The patient would then have access to the most comprehensive range of healthcare according to the most advanced standards, but this privilege would come with a financial ruin because no buying power would be left for any other expenses beyond the medical expenditures. The healthcare system in its present form moves towards this absurdity.

In education, the situation is similar, albeit with a different emphasis. Both education and health are so-called superior goods, where the demand rises more than proportional to income. This would be no problem if the beneficiary of the product were to bear the costs. It is different, however, with health and education. The recipients of the service are not the same who pay. An excessive demand is a result. Over-consumption occurs with both, health and education. The costs are exploding because neither from the buyer nor on the side of the supplier is a wedge in place. Demand is individual, but the costs are borne by the collective of the insured. The logic of the system drives to its expansion and to rising costs.

While individual consumption ceases when the marginal utility no longer covers the marginal costs in the case that the recipient pays the price, consideration of benefits and costs play almost no role in the demand and supply of education and health. Here, the beneficiaries continue to consume even if the additional costs exceed the marginal benefit. Goods like education and health have no natural saturation points. Since finding the optimum is not an option, the demand moves to the maximum. Even if each patient had his personal physician, there would be further demand. This is also the case with education. Demand shifts from the optimum to the maximum and questions such as why not give each student his own special teacher appear no longer absurd. When healthcare and education are apparently free, supply will never satisfy demand. Over the past several decades, it has become almost an obligation for the young to go to college – even for those who neither want it nor who are qualified for a university that deserves its name. The absence of the price system has eliminated cost control.

The interaction of demand and supply works no longer as an equilibrating process but as an accelerator toward an avalanche of expenditures. If everyone were a self-payer, the providers would have to focus on the financial capacities of the individual. Medical progress would take different paths from those which are happening now. In the same way, the role of universities and schools as diploma factories would have long since disappeared, and different forms of education would have emerged if there were a free market in this area. Yet because the state acts as a provider that apparently delivers the goods for free, alternative suppliers cannot effectively compete. Because of the quasi-monopolistic position of the public educational agencies, the offers from private suppliers are crowded-out. The supply of alternatives shrinks although these would be better and cheaper than the official provision. The same applies to modern medical practices, where the potential for cost saving remains under-used since no significant incentives for efficiency exist.

A free capitalism would end with the collectivism that prevails in the education and health system. Disposable income would rise, and people could spend it according to one's personal preferences - different from the present system where one must pay for the use about which the contributor has little if any say. As with healthcare, the costs of education exceed the marginal benefits. Consequently, the services become more comprehensive and more expensive. In the educational system, the larger the proportion of people in each cohort who go to college and the higher the formal level of education of this group, the more the relative costs per pupil and student increase while their qualifications sink.

Cost Explosion in Education

The rise of the costs of the American educational system began when 'education insurance' became the norm according to which students gained easy access to government-subsidized loans.

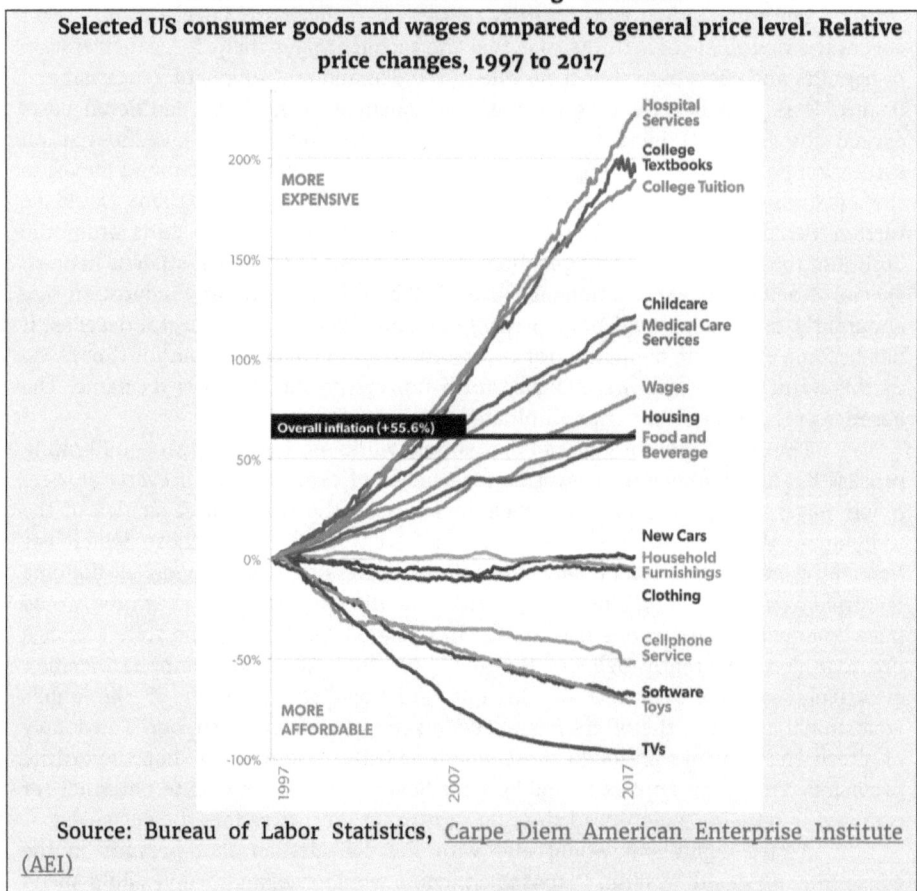

Costs and benefits of college education

Source: Bureau of Labor Statistics, Carpe Diem American Enterprise Institute (AEI)

This system came about because the education policy did no longer focus on the best education as an objective but on its expansion. The new aim was to have as many students as possible in college.

For the United States, the graph above shows the increase in the cost of a university education compared to the general consumer price index and to other consumer goods and services. Along with hospital costs, college education shows the highest increases. Studies that show that graduates earn higher salaries than those without studies are correct, but they ignore that this unequal distribution of income would also have come about when these more talented and dedicated persons had not attended a university.

The higher, albeit loan-financed, ability it was for the students to pay for their education, the more universities and colleges have raised prices and expanded those areas, which had little to do with the educational goal. As a result, many campuses of U.S-universities became more like sports and amusement parks than places of higher learning. As the academic program is no longer the focus of attention, but the quantity of students, the proportion of part-time instructors and substitute teachers has expanded at the expense of qualified professors. The number and salaries of those who work in the university administration rose and the incomes of the directors and coaches of the various sports teams with whom the colleges promote their 'branding' rose to astronomical levels.

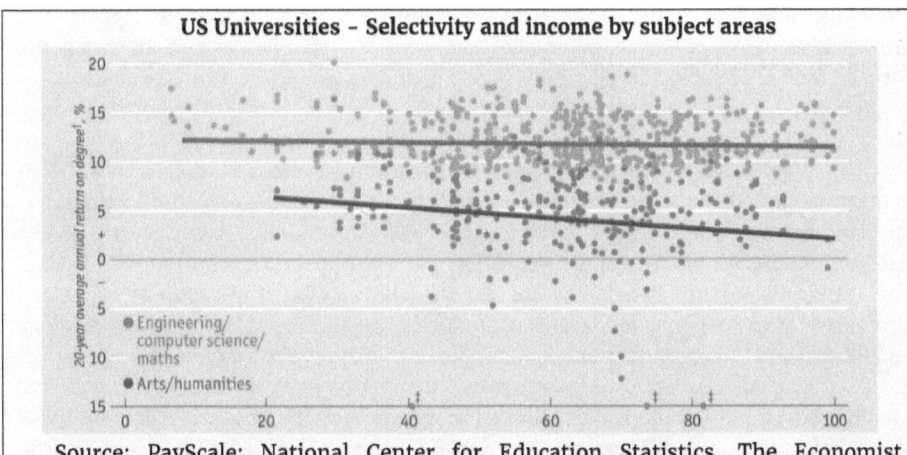

Source: PayScale; National Center for Education Statistics. The Economist
http://www.economist.com/gallery/2015-03-06/20150307-universities

The graph shows the 20-year average of the annual earnings as a percentage of the respective university degree (left scale) compared to the selectivity of the university according to the admission rate 2012-13 as a percentage of 240 institutions where the degree was obtained. The upper line: Regression line (line of best fit) for engineering sciences, computer science, and mathematics. The lower regression line for the arts and humanities.

There are no significant differences between the low-barrier colleges and the selective universities. The main difference in income comes not from where but from what one studied. Students who studied technical and mathematical disciplines earn a higher income than those who study disciplines of the humanities, irrespective of the status of the university where they have studied.

There is comprehensive evidence to show that what to study is more important than where to study. Even more so: anything that one would want to study now, is the Internet - free of charge. For education, there has never been a need for public funding, and nowadays this is even more so the case.

Studies show that getting a college degree serves as a signaling for employers. Having absolved a college serves as a sign of certain levels of discipline, intelligence, and obedience – traits, which employers do esteem and that are much more important than what one has learned at the college. Students themselves care less about what they learn than how to pass a course and to get the desired diploma. Tests confirm that students forget most of the contents of what they have studied at the schools. With some exceptions, many academic disciplines teach useless subjects.

This thesis finds support from analyses that show that the role of the 'prestige' and 'selectivity' of the educational institutions has almost no significance for salaries. It is not where one studies, but what subject one has chosen that is the crucial factor for career development in terms of salaries.

***

The problem with the modern educational system is that it has fallen almost completely under the authority of the state. Therefore, the system has become more bureaucratic as it has become less educational. Disguised as a public good of immense 'social value', education has evolved into a multi-billion dollars industry whose main benefactor are not the students but the group of organized providers of educational services. Not unlike the medical establishment, a credulous public accepts the apparent benefits of education without a trace of doubt.

Higher academic degrees serve the individual to get more personal remuneration but for the cohort, education means that one does out-compete those with lower degrees while more education for the whole group does not make the economy more productive. Tests and other types of examination do not serve as ways to find out the qualification of the candidates for doing useful work but how they match up with their colleagues in terms of such yardsticks as general intelligence, perseverance, and conformity.

The modern state-run and state-certified system of education would collapse when employers discard academic degrees as a screening device. Education would become useful when it focuses on specific skills that people can learn at specialized institutions that cooperate with firms which business finances. In a free capitalism, there is no room for state-run and union-controlled schools. People would not spend the best years of their lives as college kids but learn early on how the world works.

SOCIAL POLICY

Since its inception, social policy has been a tool to gain mass loyalty and win electoral votes. This concept was already at the heart of Bismarck's social policy when he implanted a 'white revolution' from above to fight the 'red revolution' from below in his struggle against the social democracy and the other socialist movements in the late 19th century. Today, as in the past, social policy is neither left nor right in the political spectrum, but it is a populist-nationalist project.

Under the current democracy, political parties try to outdo each other with new designs for 'social security' and 'welfare' and 'justice for all'. In politics, however, 'better' means more spending and higher costs. Therefore, these proposals come down to nothing more than to increase the costs for the general population. In the modern democracies, almost the complete population is under the cover of the social state - be it because of membership in the statutory health and pension insurance schemes or in the obligatory unemployment insurance and occupational accident insurance or because of the U.S. programs Medicaid and Medicare. In addition, there are family subsidies and child allowances, and social assistance programs.

Despite the broadening and deepening of the social programs, social issues have not diminished. Not only in the European countries, but also as to the United States, one could observe that new social policy plans have augmented the hardships and widened the number of people in need instead of reducing the social ailments and to diminish the dependency on the programs. Never in America have the poor been 'losing ground' so much as under the social welfare expansion that came with the launch of the 'Great Society' in the 1960s.

Originally, the design of social policy was for a society in which there was the family help and that of the community before the state aid and where 'to live on welfare' was a disgrace. This has changed. The traditional family associations have broken down, and the state support has become a 'human right'. While in the past, the recipient of social welfare suffered from a stigma, now, who does not take advantage of the system is the dupe.

The modern economy and society are no longer an industrial society in the traditional sense. The idea of social insurance was to protect the industrial workers. This model assumed that the employee would remain in the same field of activity and even stay in the same company until the statutory age of retirement. Additionally, the design of the social security systems presumed that the period during which a pensioner would receive the old-age pension was only a few years. As to illness and unemployment, too, the design of the system assumed these periods without own earnings from work as temporary emergencies. For this purpose, it was necessary to include the individual in a collective of solidarity and to protect the industrial worker against the financial consequences of illness, disability, unemployment, and old age.

In the modern technological society, there are less fixed and lifelong employment relationships. Horizontal and vertical mobility has become indispensable. Although workplace and society have changed, most governments still cling to the traditional concept of social policy. Yet the modern economy and society are moving away from the model of the old industrial society as it still existed in the 1950s and 1960s. The social policymakers, however, stick to the old model and wonder that the reforms do not work. The solution to the problem does not consist in reforms to maintain and expand the system but to make the system leaner and to abolish it.

The consequence of the sprawling social policy is that governments stumble from one deficit to the next, that politicians with the appropriate slogans win the election and then lose support after the voters wake up to the insight that these politicians, when they are in the government, cannot deliver what they promised in the election campaign. Then comes the next tentative, and the cycle starts again with the next election. Over time, the parties and their representatives will become more like each other and indistinguishable as to their policies when in power. Each party in power contributes in its own way to bring down the economy.

The policy is stuck in a permanent conflict of an ongoing ambivalence between too much government activities and less populism. In the first case, the economy produces less while in the second case politics does not get its share and the success at the elections wanes. The modern state is politics with an affiliated economy. Yet in a system dominated by populism, politicians come to power by squeezing the productive economy and distributing the benefits according to their political calculus. It is obvious that the productive sector of the economy does not favor this approach. The insight has been lost that the best social policy is a good economic policy and that the best economic policy is as little policy as possible or better even none.

Government spending

All industrialized countries have experienced an increase in the relative share of government expenditure as a share of the gross domestic product since the end of the 19th century.

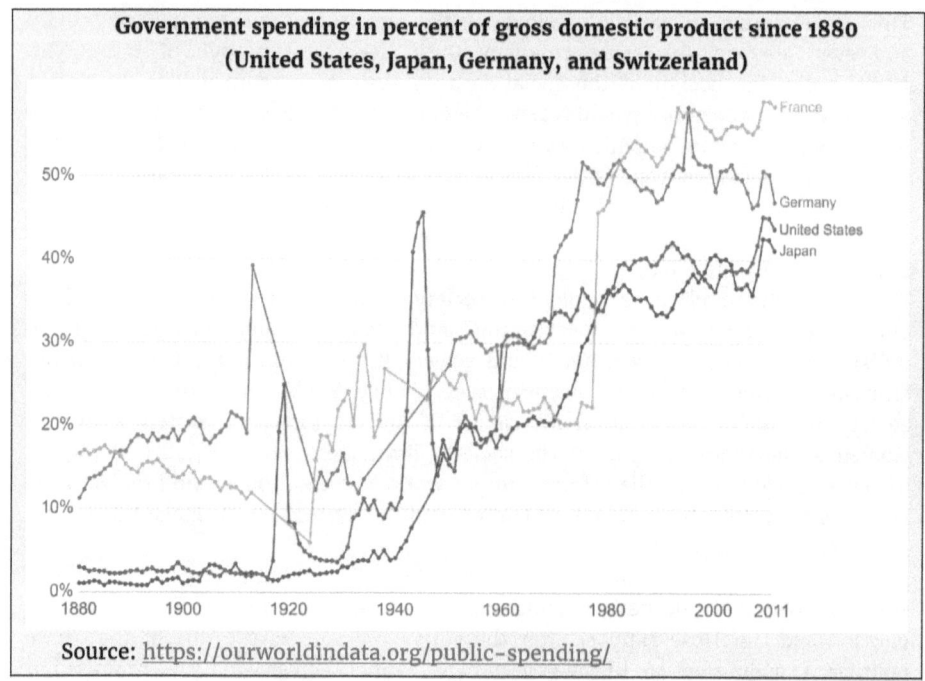

Source: https://ourworldindata.org/public-spending/

In Italy and Germany, the rate rose from around ten percent to around 50 percent, and for the United States from less than five percent to around 45 percent, and in Japan to over 40 percent. Even in Switzerland, the share of the state rose to about 35 percent. From a level of less than a tenth of gross domestic product around 1880, government spending has increased to almost half to the GDP in the 1970s in many industrialized countries.

The compilation shows that the major sources of the expansion of social government spending over the past decades have been healthcare and old age. Given that the process of aging will continue and speed up, social government spending will take a growing share in decades to come if the present system remains unchanged.

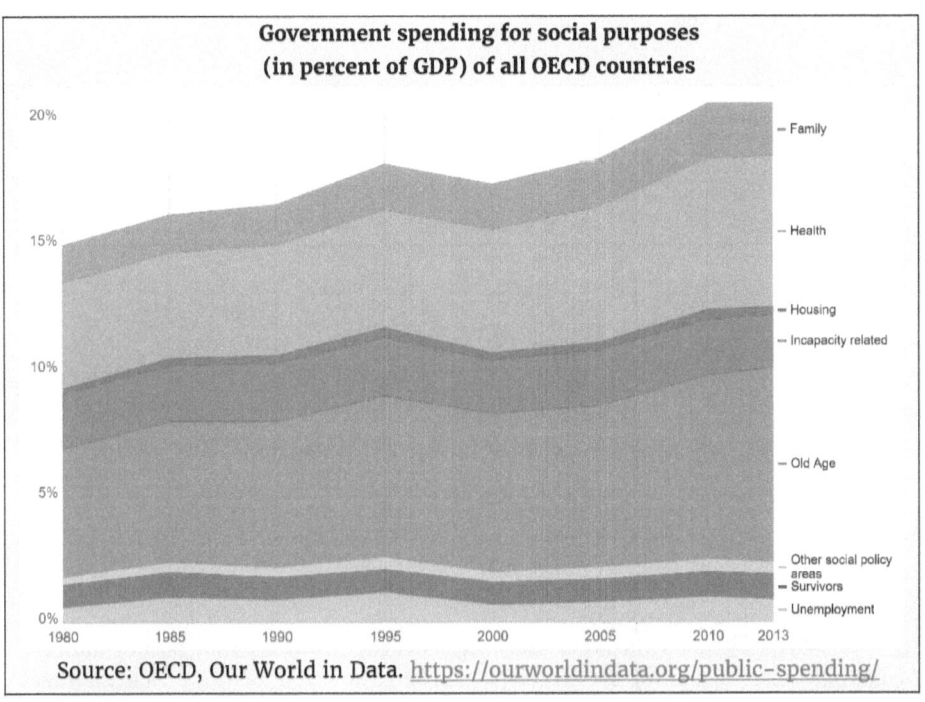

Antony P. Mueller

ORIGINS OF SOCIAL POLICY

Implementing social security systems and providing so-called welfare and social justice as governmental goals have become the outstanding features of the state since the late 19th century.

Germany is a case worth studying. This country was a pioneer in creating a comprehensive system of social policy, and it is now one of the prime examples where a maze of regulations and the fiscal burden that has come with this kind policy is paralyzing the economy. A historical analysis of the German welfare state also reveals the close link between the welfare and the warfare state.

When Otto von Bismarck (1815-1898) as Chancellor of Germany from 1871 to 1890 conceived a system of social security for the industrial workers in the late 19th century he had a clear aim in mind. Along with strengthening the geo-strategic position of the Reich, he set out to bring the industrial workers under the control of the state. Integrating the masses into the body of the unified German state was the objective, and a comprehensive social insurance system provided the means to achieve this aim.

The social policy began as national policy, and the social security system has remained an instrument to lure the citizens away from private and communitarian systems into the arms of the government. In the eyes of Bismarck, it was the state that had created national unity and this agent was also necessary to maintain the social unity by a system of mutual obligation between the state and its citizens.

Originally, Bismarck's set up social security to be specific as to its target, limited in depth, and light in terms of the financial burden for the productive sector of the economy. When the first steps were taken towards establishing a social security system in 1883 with the inception of a health insurance system and with its expansion to cover old age, working place accidents and unemployment, the maximum contribution to social security was six percent of the gross wage. Social security was limited to the new class of the industrial workers. Regular old age pensions received only persons over 70 years of age, and the payout would amount to the subsistence level.

Adolph Wagner (1835-1917) is one of the intellectual fathers of social policy. He is the author of the 'law of increasing state activity'. Wagner foresaw that the expansion of the state functions into the 'social era' would change the character of the state and lead to an ongoing financial expansion of governmental activity. He predicted that the new 'social epoch' would be the age of interventionism when the governments would 'correct' the capitalist process of production and distribution.

While the practice and institutional forms of social policy vary from country to country, the idea that the government must protect and promote social justice and progress has become the paramount modern ideology. Following in the footsteps of Bismarck, the construction of social policy systems has emerged as the distinctive feature of the modern state.

Periods of war, depression and prosperity alike were the major propellants to expand the system when social policy became the favorite means to offer the carrot along with the stick of governmental control. Social policy ushered the way into the age of the unfettered growth of taxation, government expenditures, and bureaucracy -making the modern welfare state totalitarian as a guardian of the individual from the cradle to the grave.

In accordance with its historical roots, social policy has maintained its nationalistic aims, its paternalistic schemes, and its authoritarian practice. As such, the social policy represents the modern complement to the traditional role of the state as an agency of warfare. Social security has served as a formidable instrument in the hands of governments to obtain popular loyalty and the allegiance of special interest groups. Under democratically elected governments and dictatorships alike, the temptation has been the same: expanding the coverage of social security and of welfare has been the foremost instrument in search of government power and presumed state legitimacy.

In Germany, it was first during World War I and its aftermath, and later under the Third Reich in the 1930s when the welfare state experienced its greatest expansions. Under the national-socialist regime, the appeal to 'social justice' and to expand the social security systems flourished, together with the buildup of the warfare state. In the first couple of years of the Nazi dictatorship, social policy was one of the major legal projects of codification to create an all-encompassing 'social state'. The systematization of social policy was so profound that almost all major bodies of law that rule Germany's current social security system go back to their original formulation in the national-socialist era. While minor adaptations happened to fit the current needs, the original spirit of the social policy laws lives on with its roots in the class distinctions and the paternalistic-authoritarian schemes of the past.

Under the Third Reich, social policy measures extended to protect and promote ideologically defined standards of reproduction, health, and the environment. The carrot of social policy served as the main means to facilitate the application of the stick of repression. It also happened in this period that the labor market came under the control of the totalitarian state making the dismissal and hiring of personnel dependent on governmental permission (issued by the local Labor Office).

Grown for over a period of more than a hundred years, the various branches of the obligatory social security system have put the entire population under intensive bureaucratic care. Social policy has become a labyrinth formed by laws and regulations, individual judicial decisions and cases of special considerations that make it impossible to determine who are the net payers or who are the net beneficiaries.

The coverage of old age, sickness, and unemployment insurance, along with social aid, and disability insurance and with all the numerous special branches of social policy have become an Eldorado for those seeking a free ride. Often described as 'generous', the German social welfare system provides a plethora of incentives for becoming unemployed, seeking early retirement and fulfilling the requirements to become eligible for social aid and disability payments.

By promoting 'social progress', the modern welfare state has dissolved all limits to the governmental constraint. Together with the traditional goals of protection and social justice, the extension to social progress has opened the way to all kinds of absurdities, abuses, and interventions.

With social policy becoming ever more comprehensive, it has turned into a severe and suffocating burden for the economy. The boon—however great or small it may have been in its early stages for a specific group—has turned into a plague. Now, the dismantling of the welfare state emerges as the major policy challenge of the 21st century.

MISSING STANDARDS

It is a common misunderstanding to allow the state to take over the areas where the market economy apparently cannot work well. Expecting that through regulation the performance would improve, is the grand illusion of our time. Interventionist economic theory invented the concept of 'public' goods and 'merit' goods as different categories besides private goods. This classification claims there are goods whose usefulness is unrecognized by the individual consumer and therefore requires extra incentives that increase their consumption.

These 'merit goods' do not share the characteristics of a public good such as non-excludability and non-rivalry of consumption but are like private goods. The presumed systematic under-consumption of these goods requires state intervention. As if it were a matter of fact, the state takes over health care and education, jurisprudence, and security on the assumption that there is no other alternative. Even if it were the case that these goods are 'public' and 'merit', the problem arises by which standards production and distribution should take place when markets instead of the market, the state operates in these areas.

The regulatory state eliminates competition where it is in place, as it is the case, for example, in the financial sector, yet at the same time introduces an artificial competition where it does not fit, as it is the case with medicine and education. This way, the economic competition gets a bad name and the market economy is discredited because the market mechanism apparently does not work in these areas when in fact the market mechanism was never meant to work here. State intervention does not cure the proclaimed market failure but makes matters worse.

When the state assumes the allocation in areas such as medical care, the individual provider of medical services no longer places the patient in the center but the bureaucratic regulations of the provider of health insurance because this is the place from where the doctors and the other suppliers of healthcare services receive their financial remuneration. The performance criterion shifts from the therapeutic success to the number of points that the respective insurance company stipulates. The patient is the loser. He rarely notices this scheme, and if one does, he does not care much, because one must pay the contribution anyway and therefore one is interested in regaining the largest part out from the obligatory payments. As everybody does so, costs explode, and the contributions rise.

State activity requires justification and faces the problem of how one can justify state intervention. One tries to solve this task by objectifying the value of a good albeit value is subjective. In the private sector, each one assesses individually the benefits of a good or service according to one's own discretion. There is no such guideline for the public sector. Before the state took over such areas as education and health, they were under the care of private charitable and religious organizations. Churches, for example, were such institutions, which consciously cultivated altruism and charity.

Before the state came to dominate these systems, there were also numerous private associations, which provided social services for specific groups. The members themselves of these private associations controlled the operations of the institution. Expanding education, healthcare, and social aid to the dimensions of the modern territorial state, the contributors have lost the knowledge about the specific trade-off between costs and benefits. People lose their status as members of the association and to become mere numbers relevant only as paying contributors. They can no longer exert effective control over the system, which has taken on a dynamic of its own. The more the state spends for healthcare, public assistance, and education, the more these areas become bureaucratic madhouses.

The usurpation by the state means that private spontaneous aid and private initiative suffer from the crowding-out by the state. When this has happened, and the bad outcomes show up, public opinion now says that the state must intervene even more because there is no alternative as there is no private supply. Yet it was the usurpation by the state that destroyed private social services since the start of the welfare state at the end of the 19th century.

Publicly funded research policy no longer aims primarily at gaining knowledge, but it is about output as defined by the norms that the state has imposed. Public medicine is no longer about healing but is concerned mainly with medical measures. Public schooling is not about education, but the concern has shifted to the score and the position in domestic and international rankings of the educational institution be it a school or a university. The result of these interventions is to abandon the original objectives in favor of - often meaningless - bureaucratic indicators.

This process occurs slowly and even the members of the apparatus themselves hardly notice it. Professors then spend a major part of their time developing research assignments and producing expert opinions for the research projects of their colleagues instead of doing own research and care for good teaching. Physicians no longer focus their diagnoses and therapy measures to heal their patients, but rather modify their activities according to the rules of financial compensation that the health care institutions stipulate. Education disappears from the school plans while the new standards come from the measurement systems of achievement as a means to climb up to the ladder of the rankings.

That the state could do better because the market economy does not do well, is a common error. In fact, free competition can also coordinate supply and demand where the market economy in the narrow sense, i.e. the price system, does not work perfectly. Competition can provide the so-called public and merit goods among the providers – different from the state, which acts as a monopoly. It is not true that there is no education without a state or no roads would be built without government spending. Public opinion laments the broad failure of the supply of goods and services under the state but takes it as a given while even small problems with private providers meet immediately the stain of a market failure with the consequent request that the government must jump in with state intervention. Throughout history, different religious groups and other non-state organizations have competed with one another to provide goods and services that have public characteristics and the features of merit goods. Over the past century, the state has wiped-out these services and established itself as a monopoly.

The state has become an obstacle to social progress. Under government tutelage, social policy has lost its original meaning and purpose. Social policy is a prominent example of the general law according to which bureaucratic organizations continue to operate the same way as before even if their original function has been lost over time.

THE CHIMERA OF SOCIAL JUSTICE

The 'march through the institutions' on the part of the cultural Marxists not only intends to undermine the political parties but also, in addition to the school system and the media, the judiciary. The judiciary is the area where the infiltration of the cultural Marxists has advanced and has grasped many who are not an active part of the movement. The judiciary has become a force that no longer promotes freedom but stifles and strangles individual freedom and the private initiative. No longer is liberty the guiding principle of jurisprudence, but 'social justice', 'social protection', and 'social inclusion'.

The concept of 'social justice' has become the substitute for communism and socialism. Because these terms suffer from negative connotations and even the word 'left' incites no longer much attraction, today's communists hide behind the concept of 'social justice'. Social justice is an invocation. It is the keyword to practice the terror of 'political correctness' and thus to suppress the freedom of expression as a preparation to eliminate all other liberties as well. Social justice is neither definable nor can it be realized. This opens the door to interventionism because social injustice lurks everywhere. In one way or another, ultimately everything is 'socially unjust'.

As soon as interventionism seemingly eliminates one aspect of the manifold appearance of injustice, new injustices show up, which equally demand urgent elimination. If it is no longer about women's rights, then the lesbians need care; and when it is no longer about the poor, another disadvantaged group needs assistance. If it is no longer the poor of the own nation, it must be those of the world that require compassion and help in the name of social justice. The zeal of those who have put social justice on their flag never rests, for their principal goal is not prosperity for all but to gain power, to realize their idea of communism, which is the deeper motive of this movement.

The way toward the rule of the cultural Marxists is the moral corruption of the people. To accomplish this, the mass media and public education must not enlighten but confuse and mislead. The media and the educational establishment work to put one part of the society against the other part. The list of the identification specifications gets larger while the groups' catalog of victimization and history of oppression becomes more detailed. To become a recognized victim of suppression is the way to gain social status and to gain the right to special assistance and to get social inclusion.

The demand for social justice creates an endless stream of expenditures deemed essential - for health, education, old age, and for all those people who are 'needy', 'persecuted' and 'oppressed', be it real or imaginary. The flood of never-ending spending in these areas corrupts the state finances and produces fiscal crises. This helps the Neo-Marxists to accuse 'capitalism' of all evils when, in fact, it is the regulatory state that provokes the systemic failures and when in fact it is the excess of public debt that causes the financial fragility.

Politics, the media, and the judiciary never pause at waging the new endless wars: the war on drugs or against high blood pressure or the campaigns that assert the struggle against obesity. The list of the enemies grows every day when one item gets dropped, new enemies such as fat, butter, eggs, and salt are on the list along with racism and xenophobia. The next stage, which is already in full preparation, is the war against one's own opinion. While the public tolerates an increasingly disgusting exposition of behavior, particularly under the cult of art, the list of prohibited words and opinions grows daily. Public opinion must not go beyond a few well-defined positions. Yet while the public debate impoverishes, the diversity of radical opinion flourishes in the hidden. From there, the counterrevolution will come – as a rebellion at the risk of a civil war.

***

The cultural Marxists drive society morally into an identity crisis by the means of the false standards of a hypocritical ethics. The aim is no longer the 'dictatorship of the proletariat', because this project has failed, but the 'dictatorship of political correctness' whose supreme authority lies in the hands of the cultural Marxists. As a new class of priests, the guardians of the 'politically correct' rule the institutions whose power they sneakily try to extend over all parts of the society. The moral destruction of the individual is a necessary step to accomplish the final victory.

It is the hallmark of all ruling groups to know how to hide their true power behind the pretense of a legitimate function, which gets the name 'justice'. Yet history demonstrates that no deceptive power lasts forever. If the rule is not yet total, and this is rarely possible, counter forces are at work to topple the ruling group, typically through a movement whose battle cry is 'freedom'. In this respect, we are at the final stage of a struggle, at the end of which either a new totalitarianism or more freedom will emerge. In the universities, the triumph of cultural Marxism is the most advanced. From the young people, the counter movement must start, or it will never come.

CONCEPTS OF JUSTICE

People are different from each other beginning with age, sex, and physical appearance. The difference among people is the foundation of society. If we all were equal, societal interchange and the economic transaction would make no sense. In this perspective, individual differences form the basis of society. We come together not despite, but because we differ from each other.

The principle of reciprocity lies at the heart of social relations. A society that systematically violates fair dealings cannot survive and will not prosper. This also holds for the procedural justice which requires fair play and restorative justice, which demands the compensation of wrongs. While these principles are essential for the maintenance and progress of society, distributive or social justice is ambivalent. In a strictly philosophical sense, it remains problematic to justify social justice as a right. While the principles of reciprocal justice refer to the relationship of person to person, with the procedural justice to the dispute resolution among dissenting individuals, social justice has no individual as its basis but refers of the right of a group against society. This deviance makes 'social justice' a tricky and a false construct.

'Social justice' is a notion that one can fill at will with all kinds of claims. In the light of social justice, injustice is universal. Once that social justice is taken seriously, there is no end to the claim that society is obliged to manage the many ailments that anyone can bring forth in the name of the idea of social justice.

Because there is no such thing as social justice and never will be, the social justice movement works against society. Social justice is a hierarchical concept as it does not refer to the relations among equals but to the relationship of submission. Yet who is the suppressor? The society as a whole?

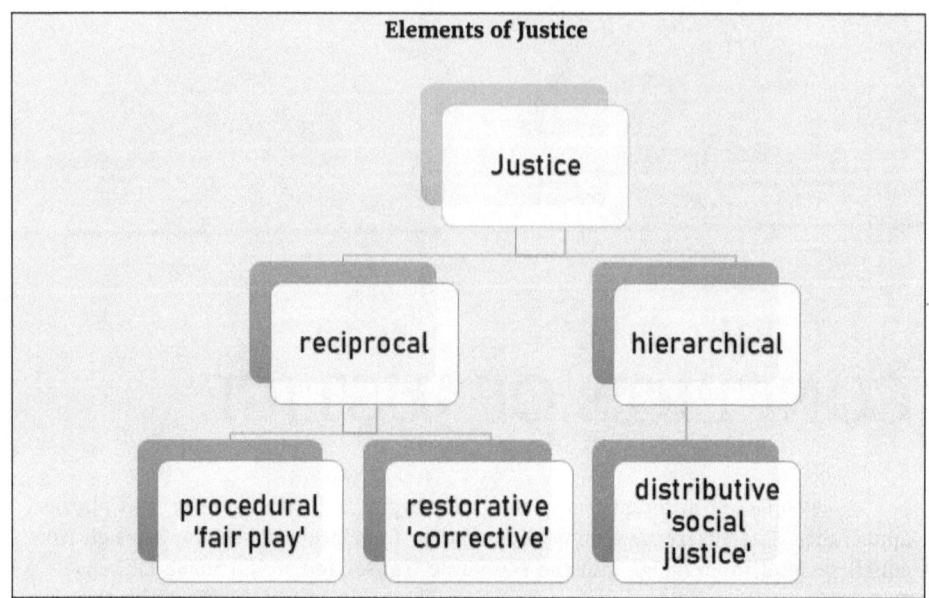

IV.

PERPETUAL FISCAL AND MONETARY CRISES

The economics of the public debt -
Where does the money come from? -
Capital, savings, and entrepreneurship -
Summary

The result of interventionism is a weaker economic performance. The other factor is government debt, which also contributes to lower the economic output. Not only in Greece and the other southern Eurozone countries, but also in the United States, Germany, and in Japan, government debt is moving steadily toward the collapse. Governments will not diminish indebtedness voluntarily without the urgent need that comes in the form of financial crisis. As soon as the gap between spending and revenue closes again because the economic situation is improving, new spending plans come into action. While the long-term trend towards more spending continues, revenues erode. Governments pursue a policy of debt financing so long as they legally and practically can. The question is not resolved by stipulating that there are limits to government spending. The fact is that governments spend as long and as much as they can. They do this to the extent that they can finance the budget deficits. Consequently, the discrepancy between spending and receipts increases while the government's funding needs are rising. This will go on until the debt collapse has become unavoidable.

U.S. government debt is on the rise since the 1970s. It experienced two accelerations. The first happened after the start of the new millennium and the second one after the financial crisis of 2008. In December 2017, U.S. government reached a new high of 20,6 trillion US-dollars.

The chart shows the evolution of government debt ratio from its height at the end of World War II. In the 1950s and 1960s, the decrease of government debt came along with strong economic growth, which lasted until the 1970s. A new boost of public debt occurred from the mid-seventies to the mid-nineties, while the second big expansion of government debt took place after the turn of the millennium and has continued until today.

At the end of 2017, government debt reached 106% of the U.S. gross domestic product. After its fall from a high of 122% in 1946 to a low of 32% in 1974, the ratio rose again since the early 1980s and attained a new boost up to the current height after the financial crisis of 2008.

Official projections say that the U.S. federal debt per person will reach 70,000 dollars by 2019. After the rise in the 1980s, the debt level plateaued somewhat in the 1990s to take off again at the beginning of the new millennium and experiencing a dramatic increase since the financial crisis of 2008 from 30,000 to 60,000 dollars per capita in 2017.

***

Eventually, the relentless logic of government debt takes hold that one can no longer sustain the debt burden as economic growths will weaken because of the public debt. In addition to old debt and new borrowing, the level of the interest rate, the inflation rate, and the growth rate of national output determine the debt ratio (debt as a percentage of the gross domestic product). The debt ratio augments with new debt and when interest rates rise. The rate of government debt declines, the faster the economy grows. With growth is too low, the price inflation comes into play as a way out. Inflation and hyperinflation reduce the real burden of the debt. The government can avert official state bankruptcy through hyperinflation, yet this means the expropriation of the savers and the ruin of the national economy.

In many industrialized countries, the financial crisis goes hand in hand with a demographic predicament. The system of statutory pension insurance makes having children costly (in terms of opportunity costs) and thus is self-destructive. The collective pension insurance compels a young couple that wants to raise children to bear not only the cost of child-rearing but also to forgo a salary. With a part of the income lost, subsequent pension claims diminish in contrast to the couple that has no children and continues to receive two incomes and consequently gains two pension claims. The system of statutory pension insurance proves that the welfare state is suicidal. The welfare state eats its own children and grandchildren.

The specific problem of government debt results from the fact that government credit is unhinged from the productive capacity of the national economy. The status of government debt differs from private debt. The analysis of creditworthiness for a company limits the loan to the profitability of the company's projects. The debt capacity depends on the company's capability of generating profits that are high enough to pay interest and principal. Likewise, a consumer credit depends on the extent to which the applicant has income and how the lender assesses the borrower's future income situation. With the state, it is different. The state lives from the taxes at the expense of the population. What distinguishes the state as a debtor from the other debtors is the power of the state to exert its monopoly to tax by physical force. Not only that, the state also has the right to determine which money is valid to serve as the legal tender in its territory. The state has the authority over to produce money even if the central bank is autonomous. By lifting the amount of money from its anchor in gold and silver, the modern state is de facto more absolute than the state was under absolutism – most prominently in monetary affairs.

A sovereign debt crisis is a credit crisis and at the same time a currency crisis. How the money system depends on credit shows up in the fact that the modern money emerges as a credit at is the source as the commercial banks borrow currency at a nation's central bank. The commercial banks are indebted to the central bank where they obtain cash and general liquidity. On this basis, then, the commercial banks create additional money by granting loans to their customers, including the state.

The modern state-money is a currency without an intrinsic value and without an anchor to a specific economic good, such as gold, for example. The modern monetary system has no anchorage outside the state power to implement its will by force. If the tax revenue does not rise, the state privilege of money creation will produce money at the government's discretion. Instead of a tax on income and consumption, the government raises an inflation tax by increasing the amount of money.

Antony P. Mueller

THE ECONOMICS OF THE PUBLIC DEBT

The size of a country's total public debt results from past budget deficits. A budget deficit comes into existence when a government spends more than it collects as revenue. If taxes and other sources of government receipts fall short of public spending, the government needs to borrow. With each new budget deficit, the size of debt increases and along with the principal the obligation to pay interest also rises.

As an indicator of the debt burden serves the so-called 'debt coefficient', which relates the government's overall debt to the country's gross domestic product (GDP). In the light of this number, a rise of total debt need not necessarily denote an increase of the relative debt burden. If the total debt rises together with national income, relative debt as measured by the debt coefficient remains constant. By the same token, the relative debt burden would increase even without new debt if national production should shrink.

Public debt ratios of selected countries
(Public debt in percent of gross national product as of December 2016)

Country	Public debt in percent of gross national product as of December 2016
Japan	250.4
Greece	179.0
Italy	132.6
United States	106.1
France	96.0
United Kingdom	89.3
Euro Area	89.2
Brazil	69.5
Germany	68.3

Source: National data. tradingeconomics.com

The distinction between the so-called 'primary deficit' and that part of the budget deficit, which pertains to interest payments, is important because the amount of interest payments varies not only with the size of outstanding debt but also with the interest rate.

When assessing the debt burden, the rate of price inflation makes up an important factor. Price inflation devalues outstanding debt. This happens slowly when inflation rates are low and rapidly when inflation rates are high. In the case of hyperinflation, even a gargantuan public debt would evaporate. However, a deliberate fabrication of hyperinflation to get rid of the debt burden is not a rational strategy because such a policy would come along with the collapse of the economy.

In order to capture the impact of the price level on the debt burden, one must distinguish between the nominal rate and the real rate of interest. The current nominal interest rate comprises the real interest rate plus the expected inflation rate. While the real interest rate is relatively stable, the expected inflation rate and therefore nominal interest rates are volatile because if the uncertainty concerning the future inflation rate.

Public debt in terms of the debt coefficient – total debt in percent of gross domestic production – will rise or fall according to the movement of the following determinants.

The debt coefficient as overall debt in percentage of gross domestic product will rise (+) and fall (−) with the following variables

	Debt coefficient (public debt per gross domestic product) Rises: + Falls: −
More government spending	+
Less government spending	−
More government revenue	−
Less government revenue	+
Higher interest rate	+
Lower interest rate	−
Price inflation	−
Price deflation	+
Higher economic growth	−
Lower economic growth	+

Representing the impact of the variables on the debt coefficient with a plus sign (+) for the increase and the negative sign (−) for a reduction, one can summarize these findings in the following table.

According to the enumeration above, it may appear easy to construct a package for bringing down the debt burden without cutting expenditures. Such a simplistic plan would include measures to

- raise taxes
- decrease the interest rate
- increase price inflation
- stimulate economic growth
- reduce the size of accumulated debt (by forgiveness or default)

The problem with such a policy is that while each measure would work in isolation, the factors are interdependent. Therefore, such a package would contain contradictory measures.

Determinants of the debt burden		
The relative debt burden will be higher the more		
government spends	interest ratesl rise	there has been debt accumulation in the past
The relative debt burden will be lower the more		
tax revenue increases	price inflation rises	economic growth increases

Taxes: A government cannot simply raise taxes. All it can do is to impose the tax rate. Higher tax rates do not imply higher tax revenue. A rate that is too high will lead to a lower tax revenue.

Interest rates: Central banks control the nominal interest rate for short maturities by setting the policy rate such as the federal funds rate in the case of the United States. The monetary authorities have much less power over the interest rate for longer maturities. An additional limitation of interest rate policy comes from the fact that when nominal interest rates hit zero-bound, price deflation would mean rising real interest rates.

Inflation: The monetary authorities can push the monetary base but the size of money in circulation results from the interaction of borrowers and lenders in the financial markets.

Economic growth: The long-term rate of economic growth depends on factors beyond manipulation by fiscal and monetary policies. Economic growth results from a confluence of hard and soft factors that include the quality of macroeconomic management, governance, and culture. Education, infrastructure and the legal framework exert their influence on economic growth over decades.

Debt reduction: One way to reduce the amount of past debt accumulation is debt forgiveness or default. Such a measure reduces the amount of the outstanding debt right away and lowers the coefficient. A well-negotiated debt reduction may contribute to lower interest rates and speed up an economic recovery. Economic expansion would mean an increase of government revenue particularly when it comes along with lower interest payments. Yet granting debt forgiveness and managing an orderly debt restructuring depends on the willingness of the lenders. Whether lenders agree on rescheduling to reduce the debt burden depends not only on financial factors but very much on the geostrategic position of the indebted country when foreign lending is involved as it is mostly the case with public debt.

Default: Another way of reducing the amount of current debt is by default. Yet deliberate nonpayment provides no way out of the debt trap. Such a policy would give up access to the capital market and crush economic growth right away. Any kind of default exacerbates a return to prosperity. The detrimental impact of default on economic growth may be long-lasting. As easy as it is to lose confidence as hard is it to regain trust.

***

An effective debt reduction strategy, which would bring down the debt coefficient, must address both variables of the debt quotient. Such a policy must seek to bring down total debt combined with lifting the rate of economic growth. It makes no sense to bring down debt when at the same time the economy would shrink, and the gross domestic product would fall. Likewise, the relative debt burden would not go away even with a larger gross domestic product, when the boost of economic growth rates has come mainly from more public spending. To bring down the debt coefficient, one needs to reduce absolute debt and have a growing economy.

The way to bring down total debt is to cut spending in combination with higher rates of economic growth which would require a boost in private investment. Only a very superficial analysis would point to lower interest rates as the way to get more investment. Confidence, secure property rights, and a positive profit outlook are the keys. If the central bank forces down interest rates to stimulate more investment, it will provoke investment errors. Because of the resulting economic distortions due to these malinvestments, such a kind of economic growth would not be sustainable.

In order to achieve debt reduction, spending cuts must be accompanied by an improvement of the investment climate for private enterprise. This happened after the end of World War II in the Western world when less military spending went hand in hand with a return to the principles of free markets. Different from Roosevelt's anti-capitalist rhetoric that had prolonged the Great Depression and the government's political sway over the war economy that has suppressed free enterprise, the decades after World War II saw the return to capitalist economic principles and economic growth accelerated despite massive budget cuts.

The failure of a country such a Greece to bring down the debt quotient results from the fact that the various Greek governments before and after the debt crisis have failed to coalesce the policy of spending cuts with adequate measures to increase private business confidence and to liberate the economy. Greece is the exemplary case how the march towards the debt crisis begins as a joy ride and ends in a horror trip. The higher the debt burden, the harder it is to restrain its future growth. Passing through the limit from the manageable to the unmanageable size of public debt goes with little notice. It is only after the barrier is broken that the trouble begins. Then it is often too late for a turnaround. The ride over the cliff into state bankruptcy happens as if programmed once the critical threshold is crossed.

Theory and evidence show that to overcome a debt crisis, the policy must combine the debt reduction program with incentives for private enterprise to fill up quickly and efficiently the space that the retreat of government opens. With the right incentives in place, private business will generate employment and income not despite but because the government cuts spending. The task ahead not only for the US but for all countries which are in a debt trap is to bring down debt in combined with a forceful surge towards free enterprise.

***

A loan is worth as much as the borrower can serve it by paying interest and principal. If the state can no longer finance its debt through tax revenues, it must make new debts to pay the old debts, and the confidence in the value of the money dissipates. Eventually, there will be a loss of trust in the currency, and the monetary system moves towards its collapse. Modern money as a legal tender has no value in use, only an exchange value. The acceptance of money rests on the confidence that money maintains its purchasing power and serves for the proximate spending acts. When this confidence falters, money loses its value. A reform must be fundamental: the money system itself.

A free capitalism requires abolishing the monetary monopoly of the state and the central bank. The way to do this is to legalize a competitive private monetary system. Free capitalism requires separating state and money not much different as in earlier times classical liberalism demanded the separation of state and church. Attempts to deal with government debt by proclaiming spending cuts are doomed to fail. One can curb the Moloch state only if one blocks its access to money creation. This requires that the system of public money must return into private hands.

WHERE DOES MONEY COME FROM?

The basis of the circulating money is the creation of the money base by the central bank.

The monetary base reflects the stock of foreign exchange reserves while the largest part comprises credit of the central bank to the commercial banks.

The central bank money of the commercial banks (banknotes) comes into circulation through credit, i.e. by the borrowing of commercial banks from the central bank. On this basis, the commercial banking system creates book money (also known as depositary money) by granting credits to businesses, the consumers and to the government.

The demand for credit by companies and consumers and by the state authorities at the commercial banks leads to additional money, which economic agents use for a bank transfer in the form of bank deposits and which can be converted into cash in the form of notes.

Stylized central bank balance sheet

Assets	Liabilities
Foreign currency reserves	Circulation of cash (notes)
Loans to commercial banks	Deposits of commercial banks
Bonds and other titles	Deposits of government agencies
Loans to government agencies	

Stylized commercial bank balance sheet

Assets	Liabilities
Foreign currency reserves	Circulation of cash (notes)
Loans to commercial banks	Deposits of commercial banks
Bonds and other titles	Deposits of government agencies
Loans to government agencies	

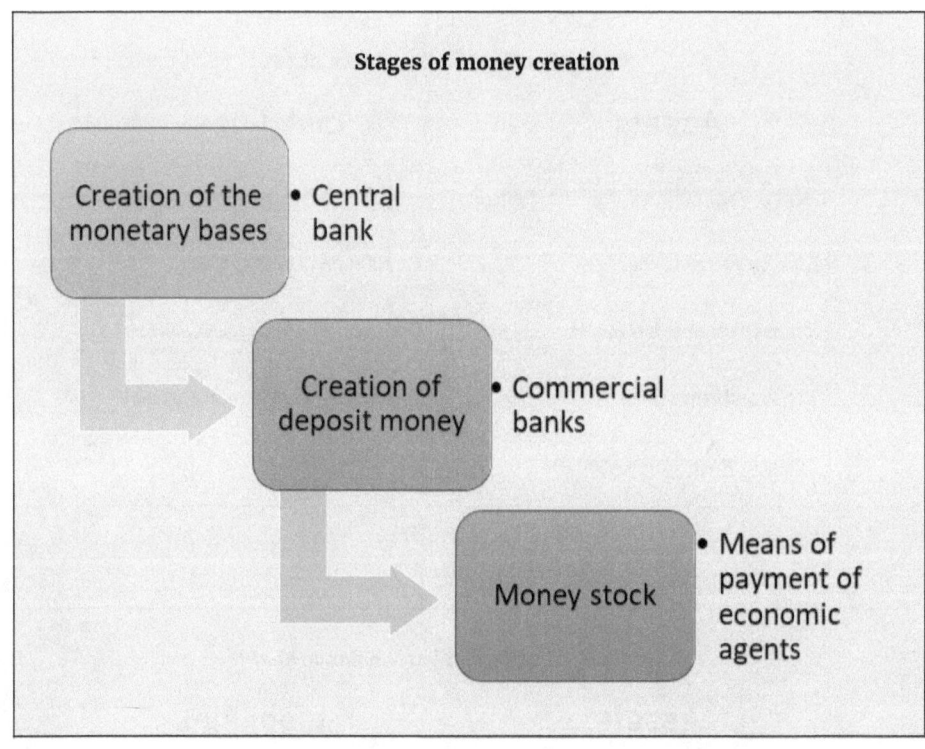

MONEY AND ASSETS

Money is the asset with the highest degree of liquidity. Money gives the holder the immediate general ability to pay. Shares, debt securities, and insurance policies have lower liquidity as they do not provide an immediate payment ability. With these assets, one must sell the titles to raise money. How much money a bond or share can generate at a specific moment is subject to fluctuations.

There are two main money producers: the central bank and the commercial banks. Both institutions create money out of thin air through the act of lending.

The statistical calculation of the asset distribution among the population, which provokes so often heated discussion, can be nothing more than a blurry snapshot because beyond cash all other assets fluctuate in price.

Stock prices are constantly changing during trading hours and are experiencing considerable changes at certain times.

For real estate, there is no market price at all comparable to that of equities. In the case of real estate, prices fluctuate, too, yet, as each object is a single piece and as such, only partially substitutable, no reliable market price exists before the sale of the object.

Household goods and works of art may be valuable for the owner, but who knows their market value?

Types of assets

Property
Rising iliquidity
Household items - art - gold - real estate

Financial assets
Rising liquidity
insurance police - notes - bonds - stocks - deposit money - cash

Cash, bank deposits, bonds, and life insurance are debt securities. The holder is a creditor. These titles, including the cash, come into the circulation as credit lines. Cash arises with the central bank which lends to the commercial banks.

A small amount of cash covers the book money, which exists in the form of bank deposits. Commercial banks have more liabilities to their deposit owners than they have cash in their vaults.

Each act of lending by a commercial bank creates a chain of deposit creation as one man's spending becomes another man's income. Therefore, the amount of deposit money exceeds the amount of cash.

Monetary aggregates of the U.S. Federal Reserve System	
M2	· M1 + · Savings deposits · Time deposists of less than 100 k · Money market funds of individuals
M1	· Cash in circulation · Demand deposits · Other checkable deposists
Monetary base (MB)	· Notes and coins in circulation · Currency in bank vaults · Reserves of commercial banks at the central bank

Antony P. Mueller

CAPITAL, SAVINGS, AND ENTREPRENEURSHIP

Monetary saving is not necessarily investment, and investment is not automatically capital formation, which renders yields and could bring forth appreciation by some compound interest formula. Real capital does not exist as a homogenous lump in the sense that there is a capital stock that enters the production function to produce the national income. Real capital exists in the form of diverse capital goods, and as such, they do not represent a source of a permanent revenue. Capital goods render an income stream only insofar as they are rearranged and renewed according to the changing market conditions. Capital without entrepreneurial activity is an empty concept.

The term 'capital' as it is frequently used and applied when calculating the financial state of households, companies, or investment funds is an accounting concept. Only in terms of monetary units can capital be treated as a sum. In contrast to monetary capital, real capital, as an ensemble of diverse capital goods, cannot be added up. As the means of production, capital is a mental concept that exists in the mind of the entrepreneur who puts the capital goods in their interaction to use. The means of production wear down by rendering the yield, and they become obsolete when the production process must be altered because of the technology or demand and competition change. Real capital left to itself does not bear fruits. On the contrary, left to itself, real capital as it exists in the form of capital goods deteriorates; capital in this sense does not grow but dies. Without entrepreneurial activity, capital is just a heap of heterogeneous capital goods. Without the entrepreneur, capital is dead. It takes the entrepreneurial activity to bring capital to life and keep capital alive.

The present consumption comes from the current production. Most of the goods that one needs to satisfy the future wants cannot be pre-produced now and saved for consumption later. It will be the state of the economy at the point of time in the future when the consumption needs arise that determines the degree of meeting the new specific demands. Because future demand will differ from today's, the capital structure currently in existence will become inadequate, and it is only by constant adaptation and new capital formation that the production process will provide the flow of consumption goods in the future periods. Higher productivity now does not guarantee that its level can be maintained, or that the areas where high productivity is presently the case will be the same that will be needed in the future. In order to preserve productivity, one needs on-going entrepreneurial management. Capital maintenance and its accumulation need perpetual savings and investment and continuous re-arrangements of the capital structure under entrepreneurial guidance.

The accumulation of financial assets may be an investment from a personal perspective, but it does not necessarily mean that real capital comes into existence. Most of the stock trade is only a rotation of ownership. Even less so does the lending to government make up the acquisition of capital goods. Governments spend most of the money on salaries and other items that are mainly consumption. In terms of saving via government bonds, there is little difference between a pension scheme of pay-as-you-go and a capital-based system, because in both cases the savings of one group is consumption by another one, and no real capital formation takes place.

Under a socialist economic system, savings and investment typically come along with capital destruction. But in the capitalist countries, too, savings, investment, and economic growth can deceive as an indicator of the future performance of an economy. If it were merely aggregate investment that mattered, economic development and swift wealth creation would be easy. Poor economies could become rich in a short time by borrowing abroad; and rich economies, where sufficient savings potential is available, could deliberately choose their desired future wealth levels. Yet economic growth requires more than saving and investment, and even together with technological progress, these conditions are not enough. Only insofar as the savings get into the hands of companies that adapt to market conditions will investment contribute to future prosperity. The entrepreneurial quality of the management and the overall socioeconomic conditions determine whether the savings are put to proper use or squandered.

Popular thinking about economic growth is still strongly influenced by the productivity theory of capital, which presumes that capital generates the yield like a tree begets its fruits. In the models of high aggregate macroeconomics, saving and investment along with technological progress are the main sources of growth. In this view, more savings imply more investment, and more investment means a higher capital stock, which in turn augments future yields. To assume a proper fertility of capital is sometimes even transferred to the accumulated monetary capital as it exists as an investment portfolio, which is said to grow automatically with its returns.

Only as an accounting tool - as 'monetary capital' - can capital be measured and said to grow or to diminish. But capital in the sense of capital goods cannot be expected to grow or to be stored over time. On the contrary. Capital goods deteriorate during production and finally disappear from the process of production. It is not accumulated monetary capital that brings forth output and renders profits and interest, but only capital in real terms as a heterogeneous ensemble of capital goods, and as such, it renders yield only insofar as it is constantly remodeled by entrepreneurs who buy labor, find and employ new techniques, and adapt the structure of production to changing conditions.

An individual member of a generational cohort may improve his future wealth position in relation to the average by saving more, but it will be the state of the economy in the future that determines the general level of well-being. Individual savings will not contribute to the aim of maintaining an adequate capital structure by buying government bonds. Giving money to the government is more harmful than good because it means that the money does not go into the hand of entrepreneurs. The savings, which the government receives from the private investor helps the government to expand its activity. Therefore, buying government bonds will deteriorate the environment where the entrepreneurial spirit can thrive.

Expecting future returns from the stock market as a wealth-generation machine is as foolish an idea as the belief that the government pays for social security checks. The expectation that it is primarily financial investment now that guarantees the yields for the time to come is as illusory as to believe that more social security contributions now would guarantee higher pensions later. By concentrating on financial schemes, the focus is diverted from the real issue. Higher stock market valuations appear as real wealth creation, and it gets ignored that it is not the price of an asset that makes up wealth but the profits that come from the process of production.

There is no escape from permanent efforts to rearrange the production process. The future levels of wealth are linked to the overall conditions of the economy as it evolves over time. The need for constant renewal of real capital requires an on-going flow of funds in terms of free capital to maintain the production process. Financial assets will appreciate insofar as net savings continue to be generated in the future and as they get into the hands of able entrepreneurs. Saving and investment will be wasteful when companies are run by managers who lack foresight and prudence or when institutional settings emerge that hamper, transform, and destroy these entrepreneurial qualities.

SUMMARY

Interventionism is the scourge of our time. Interventionism cannot hold its promises. On the contrary, governmental interference in the market processes creates new problems and generates new difficulties, while at the same time it suppresses and destroys opportunities and chances of improvement. The regulatory state leads not to prosperity but to stagnation and economic decline. For the welfare state, citizens end up paying more than they get, as the actual costs rise because of the seemingly free supply and because the social apparatus brings with it a growing bureaucracy.

The expectation that the so-called 'Third Way' would lead to a social and economic paradise has not come true. Both socialism and interventionism represent failed forms of economic governance. Weakening economic activity is the consequence of interventionism; the other cause is government debt, which contributes to lower economic output. The ultimate destiny of interventionism is the financial collapse of the state. On the one hand, expenditure for one specific item leads to new spending for another item and thus public expenditure continues to rise; on the other hand, the public debt burden lowers economic performance and the tax revenue. This way, two sides squeeze the modern interventionist welfare state: falling revenue and rising expenditures.

V.

OUTLOOK

Socialism cannot bring prosperity because it destroys the market functions of private property. Under socialism, private ownership of the means of production no longer exists, and thus there are no market prices for capital goods available. Institutionally, socialism consists in abolishing the market economy and replacing it with a planned economy. By doing away with private property of the means of production, one wipes-out market information and valuation. Even if the socialist administration puts price tags on the consumer goods, and the people may own consumer goods, there is no economic orientation about the relative scarcity of capital goods.

Many supporters of socialism suppose that business management is nothing more than a kind of registration or simple bookkeeping. Vladimir Lenin believed that the knowledge of reading and writing, and some expertise in the use of the basic arithmetic operations and some training in accounting, would be enough for the conduct of business operations. The socialists promote engineering and science, but they believe that there is no need for the entrepreneur. The regime may spend heavily on education but when there is no entrepreneurial economy, the people will stay poor, nevertheless.

The socialists ignore scarcity. They assume that a plan could stipulate the allocation of goods and services according to needs and wants. Yet the planners must answer how such a plan should find its standards of valuation. Without prices and markets, there is no orientation about which factors of production are more and which are less valuable. The socialist planners have no knowledge of the costs of the production process. Without markets, the prevailing value structure remains unknown.

Supply in relation to want makes goods valuable. In a market economy, the relative prices show the degrees of scarcity. By observing the prices, the market participants receive the information that guides them to align their economic decisions to the market signals. The price system informs about relative scarcities. There is no need for a comprehensive system of detailed information about the origin and nature of the scarcity beyond the prices to make a rational decision. The price system reduces complexity for the individual decision maker to the single number of the price. In a market economy, the economic participants need only partial knowledge to act rationally. In capitalism, the motivation to gain profits and to avoid costs work as an incentive to behave rationally. In a market economy, the prices provide information and incentives simultaneously for the seller and the buyer.

All production faces the problem of an almost unlimited number of ways how to produce a good. One can manufacture a commodity with very different raw materials, technologies, and combinations of the production factors and in an endless variety of designs.

Along with the technological feasibility of a project, one must calculate its profitability. Without costs in relation to sales, a technical evaluation makes no sense. That a project is technically viable does not mean that its realization is also worthwhile. What appears efficient from a technical point of view need not be so in terms of economic expediency. With costs left out of the consideration, socialist production is blind to the risk of producing goods that cost more than they are worth. In a socialist economy, even a benevolent dictator could not provide the right mix of goods in terms of price and quality

Socialists suppose that to implant their rule on the economy all that is necessary is to socialize the private companies, replace the management, and install worker councils, and the new economic order would flourish. The early socialists expected that abundance would follow not least because now the workers would get what before went into the hands of the capitalists as profits. Yet the socialists ignored that the socialization of the means of production was just the beginning. They failed miserably in running the economy.

The error of socialist economic planning is to assume that business management could also continue as before after socialist operators take over the capitalist management. While the socialist regime can train administrators and engineers and put the party members in the position of directors, these new leaders cannot decide according to relative scarcities because there is no longer a private property-based entrepreneurial price system available.

The reality of socialism is the command and obedience. Without orientation from markets and prices, brute force rules the allocation of the goods. The claim to combine socialism and democracy is as much a fraud as the assertion that socialism would bring prosperity. Socialism's true face is totalitarian despotism .

It is no wonder that even a degenerate capitalism produces more prosperity than the best socialism. Therefore, the task ahead cannot be to remove capitalism in favor of socialism but to make capitalism better. In other words: make it *more* capitalist.

Antony P. Mueller

THE THREAT OF CULTURAL MARXISM

Another name for the neo-Marxism of increasing popularity in the United States is cultural Marxism." This theory says that the driving force behind the socialist revolution is not the proletariat — but the intellectuals. While Marxism has largely disappeared from the *workers'* movement, Marxist theory flourishes today in cultural institutions, in the academic world, and in the mass media. This "cultural Marxism" goes back to Antonio Gramsci (1891-1937) and the Frankfurt School. The theorists of Marxism recognized that the proletariat would not play the expected historical role as a "revolutionary subject." Therefore, for the revolution to happen, the movement must depend on the cultural leaders to destroy the existing, mainly Christian, culture and morality and then drive the disoriented masses to Communism as their new creed. The goal of this movement is to establish a world government in which the Marxist intellectuals have the final say. In this sense, the cultural Marxists are the continuation of what started with the Russian revolution.

Led by Lenin, the perpetrators of the revolution regarded their victory in Russia only as the first step to the world revolution. The Russian Revolution was neither Russian nor proletarian. In 1917, the industrial workers in Russia represented only a small part of the workforce, which mainly consisted of peasantry. The Russian Revolution was not the result of a labor movement but of a group of professional revolutionaries. A closer look at the composition of the Bolshevist party and of the first governments of the Soviet state and its repressive apparatus reveals the true character of the Soviet revolution as a project that did not aim at freeing the Russian people from the Tsarist yoke but was to serve as the launchpad for the world revolution.

The experience of World War I and its aftermath showed that the Marxist concept of the "proletariat" as a revolutionary force was an illusion. At the example of the Soviet Union, one could also see that socialism could not function without a dictatorship. These considerations brought the leading Marxist thinkers to the conclusion that a different strategy would be required to establish socialism. Communist authors spread the insight that the socialist dictatorship must come in disguise. Before socialism can succeed, the existing culture must change. Control of the culture must precede political control.

Helping the neo-Marxists was the fact many of their efforts in taking control of culture happened parallel to the encroachment of the state on individual liberties. Over the past decades, at the same time when so-called political correctness has been on the rise, the American government obtained a vast arsenal of repressive instruments. Few Americans seem to know that the U.S. is still under emergency law that has been in force since George W. Bush used the executive privilege to declare a state of national emergency in 2001. In the same year, 9/11 opened also the path to push through the Patriot Act. From a score of around 95 points, the Freedom House "Aggregate Index of Freedom" of the United States has fallen to 86 points in 2018.

The way toward the rule of the cultural Marxists is the moral corruption of the people. To accomplish this, the mass media and public education must not enlighten but confuse and mislead. The media and the educational establishment work to put one part of the society against the other part. While group identities get more specific, the catalog of victimization and history of oppression becomes more detailed. To turn into a recognized victim of suppression is the way to gain social status and to obtain the right to special assistance, of respect and social inclusion.

The demand for social justice creates an endless stream of expenditures deemed essential — for health, education, old age, and for all those people who are "needy," "persecuted" and "oppressed," be it real or imaginary. The flood of never-ending spending in these areas corrupts the state finances and produces fiscal crises. This helps the Neo-Marxists accuse "capitalism" of all evils when, in fact, it is the regulatory state that provokes the systemic failures and when it is the excess of public debt that causes the financial fragility.

Politics, the media, and the judiciary never pause at waging the new endless wars: the war on drugs or against high blood pressure or the campaigns that assert the endless struggle against fat and obesity. The list of the enemies grows every day whether racism, xenophobia, and anti-Islamism. The epitome of this movement is political correctness, the war against having one's own opinion. While the public tolerates disgusting expositions of behavior, particularly under the cult of the arts, the list of prohibited words and opinions grows daily. Public opinion must not go beyond the few accepted positions. Yet while the public debate impoverishes, the diversity of radical opinion flourishes in the hidden.

The cultural Marxists drive society morally into an identity crisis by the means of the false standards of a hypocritical ethics. The aim is no longer the "dictatorship of the proletariat," because this project has failed, but the "dictatorship of political correctness" whose supreme authority lies in the hands of the cultural Marxists. As a new class of priests, the guardians of the new orthodoxy rule the institutions whose power they try to extend over all parts of the society. The moral destruction of the individual is a necessary step to accomplish the final victory.

The believers of neo-Marxism are mainly intellectuals. Workers, after all, are a part of the economic reality of the production process and know that the socialist promises are rubbish. Nowhere was socialism established as the result of a labor movement. The workers have never been the perpetrators of socialism but always its victim. The leaders of the revolution have been intellectual party politicians and military men. It was up to the writers and artists to conceal the brutality of the socialist regimes through articles and books and by films, music, and paintings, and to give socialism a scientific-intellectual, aesthetic and moral appearance. In the socialist propaganda, the new system appears to be both fair and productive.

The cultural Marxists believe that someday they will be the sole holders of power and be able to dictate to the masses how to live and what to think. Yet the neo-Marxist intellectuals are in for a surprise. When socialism should come indeed, the "dictatorship of the intellectuals" will be anything but benign — and not much different from what happened after the Soviets took power. The intellectuals will be among the victims. This was, after all, the way as it had happened in the French Revolution, which was the first attempt of a revolution by intellectuals. Many of the victims of the guillotine were prominent intellectuals who had earlier supported the revolution — Robespierre among them.

In his play about "Danton's Death," the dramatist Georg Büchner famously had a person say: *"Like Saturn, the revolution devours its own children."* Yet more appropriately one should say that the revolution eats its spiritual fathers. The very same intellectuals who nowadays promote cultural Marxism will be the first in line if their project of conquest should succeed.

Contrary to what Marx believed, history is not pre-determined. The march through the institutions has gone far but there is not yet been a full take-over. There is still time to change course. To counteract the movement, one must note the inherent weakness of cultural Marxism. To the extent that the neo-Marxists altered classical Marxism and eliminated its basic tenets (deepening proletarianization, historical determinism, total collapse of capitalism), the movement has become even more utopian than previously socialism ever was.

As the successors of the New Left, the "democratic socialists" of the present time propagate a hodgepodge of contradictory positions. Because of the character of this movement as a promoter of group conflict, neo-Marxism is ineffectual to serve as an instrument of gaining coherent political power as it were necessary for a dictatorship. Yet this does not mean that the neo-Marxist movement has no impact. On the contrary: because of its inherent contradictions, the ideology of cultural Marxism is the main source of the profound confusion that has grabbed almost every segment of the modern Western societies and which is about to swell into even more dangerous proportions.

RUINOUS WELFARE STATE

Many people regard the welfare state as a great achievement. Yet few recognize that the larger the welfare state becomes, the more the beneficiaries themselves must bear the costs. The users must pay for what they receive and, in addition to that, they also bear the administrative expenses and must pay for the rent-seeking of special interest groups that exploit the system for their own benefits. There is a welfare and social benefits industry in place that ranges from the medical-pharmaceutical complex and the university system to the employment opportunities of social workers.

Traditionally, the relatively wealthy persons of the society have cared for the poor. Voluntary charity is a feature of all societies. Yet when the state expands into the welfare state, charity loses its meaning. The more the general population falls into the hold of the welfare state, the more diffuse the definition of need becomes and the larger the number of the contributors will grow. In the end, all pay more than they get.

Many of the evils that the voters attribute to 'capitalism' are the result of the fact that these very same citizens demand from the political parties in the election what they lament after the election. The public supply of goods that was expected to come gratis through the so-called 'social state' turns out to be more expensive than it would be under a private system. Because there is no individual direct obligation to pay for the public good, demand rises. Instead because of the individual's assessment of utility and cost, the demand for the goods and services increases because the supply is apparently free. An avalanche of costs is the necessary consequence of such a system. Prices continue to increase even when the benefits of the services sink. While costs rise, the quality of the provision falls.

In the welfare state, moral hazard is pervasive. The wider the scope of social protection and the higher the benefits, the stronger the incentives become to provoke the specific needs, which the social policies cover. The largest profiteers of the relentless expansion of the welfare state are those who produce the goods and provide the services. With health, this group is composed of the healthcare providers: the medical doctors, hospital employees, and the pharmaceutical complex. With public education, the main beneficiaries are not the pupils and students, but those who run the schools and universities. The more the system expands, the larger the benefits for the providers and the higher the costs for those who are said to be the prime beneficiaries of the 'free' public good.

Since its inception, dissatisfaction with the welfare state has increased at the same tempo as the costs of the welfare state have risen. Since its beginning, social security was sold to the public as an offer that apparently would come to the old, sick, and needy free of charge. This illusion still rules regarding the modern comprehensive welfare state. Consequently, the demand for social policies systematically exceeds the supply, even while the dissatisfaction with the performance of the system rises. An insurance, when organized as a collective system as it is the case with healthcare, brings with it that the users will ignore the principle of marginal utility and marginal costs. The gates are open to the avalanche of costs because demand rises to the saturation point.

Without a fundamental change, the healthcare Moloch in the advanced industrialized countries will absorb more and more of the income of the population. The system moves to its complete financial ruin. The absurdity looms that hardly any disposable income will be left beyond the expenditures for health, old age, social welfare, and paying taxes.

Data show that healthcare expenditures that exceed 2000 dollars per capita a year do no longer increase life expectancy. In the United States, which spends five times this amount, life expectancy is actually lower than in countries that spend less. Perverse incentives are in place that drive up the costs without an increase of benefit. This trend becomes fully insane when medical science itself says that not the expenditure for healthcare determines health and longevity, but a person's lifestyle.

In education, the situation is similar, albeit with a different emphasis. Both education and health are so-called superior goods, where the demand increases more than proportional to a rise in income. This would be no problem if the beneficiaries of the product were to bear the costs themselves. Yet as the link between the individual demand and the personal payment is cut, an excessive demand is the result. Over-consumption occurs with both, health and education. With education, a host of indicators suggests that most of the public education is not about learning but mainly about signaling. Students want a degree mainly to out-rival their cohort in the job market.

Goods like education and health have saturation points that are far beyond any reasonable limit. Demand tends forever to outstrip supply. Even if each patient had his personal physician, there would be a further demand for healthcare. This is also the case with education. Demand shifts from the optimum to the maximum and questions such as why not give each student his own special teacher to prepare every child for a PHD appear no longer absurd. When healthcare, education, and social justice become declares objectives of public policy, supply will always fall short of demand. Despite the broadening and deepening of the social programs, social issues have not diminished. In America, the poor have been 'losing ground' by the social justice and welfare expansion that came with the launch of the 'Great Society' in the 1960s. In Europe, the talk is about the 'new poverty'.

Political parties try to outdo each other with new designs for 'social security' and 'welfare' and 'justice for all'. In politics, however, 'better' means not an improvement but more spending and higher costs. Therefore, these proposals come down to nothing more than to increase taxes, contributions, and the public debt. A free capitalism would abolish the collectivism that prevails in the education and healthcare system. Disposable income would rise, and people could spend it according to personal preferences - different from the present system where one must pay without little if any say.

Antony P. Mueller

AT THE CROSSROADS

Political elections have become ideological clashes. The campaigns are not only about the next government but also about a choice between different political cultures. Although the great debate concerns no longer the alternative between communism and capitalism, the key question remains: whether society should move to more state intervention or to a market economy. This way, the traditional question of socialism or capitalism is still on the table.

<u>Populist interventionism</u> is the most widespread economic system of our time. The countries differ in degrees whether their government is less or more active in practicing interventionism. Money is under the control of the state. The state mingles in the economic transactions through taxation and regulation. While some sectors are more under state control than others, the consequence of interventionism is visible: the sectors with the persistent crises – such as the internal and external security, healthcare, old-age provision, education, money, and finance – are those, which are under the most comprehensive governmental control. A vast apparatus of subsidies sustains the defense industry, part of the automobile sector, the pharmaceuticals companies, large parts of the agriculture, and the educational institutions.

The interventionists unite with special interest groups, who cloak their specific concerns as a common good. Under interventionism, the market competition perverts into a struggle for subsidies and bailouts. The winners are no longer those who best contribute to the growth of the economy and serve the consumers, but those receive the largest share who have the best political contacts. In the end, no one is better off. In the long run, everyone is paying the price when the economy falters, including those who got a big share from the government when the economy was still flourishing.

There is a tendency to choose interventionism and move on to the road to socialism without considering which consequences will follow from this choice. Emotions and prejudices are behind the attractiveness of socialism. The socialists dream of a society where righteousness and prosperity rule together with equality of all while they prepare the opposite.

The loss of reason prepares the path for the creed in the socialist utopia. The socialization during the time of adolescence reinforces the biological disposition for socialism because children and the youngsters live under the quasi-socialist systems of the family, the schools, and the university until they are grown-up and often remain under the socialist spell for the rest of their lives. The longer these preadult periods last, the deeper becomes the socialist mentality ingrained into the psyche and minds of the young.

To break free from the socialist faith requires an act of reason or one will stay captive. One of the first steps to get deliverance from the socialist faith is the rational insight that not redistribution helps the poor, but economic growth and a free capitalism. The path to prosperity is not redistribution but productivity.

Modern democracy suffers from the contradiction that while most citizens mistrust the politicians and the state, and want fewer taxes and less state control, each voter is eager to use his vote in such a way as to get the largest piece of the cake. Such a system is neither democratic nor capitalist; it is corrupt as it produces a political game in which every single voter tries to betray all other voters. The principle of modern democracy is that while the voters try to cheat one another in getting a free lunch, the political establishment deceives all the voters.

Ironically, it was the success of capitalism that created the socialist expectation of a world without scarcity. The capitalist experience showed that a prosperous world was no longer a utopian fantasy. The early socialists were convinced that socialism would increase the productivity of capitalism not despite but because of the equality of distribution. In the socialist paradise, one could have a greater material abundance than under capitalism along with the eradication of injustices and discriminations.

The driving motif of the early socialist movement was idealism. Today, the drive is materialistic. The state should become the great provider, be it public transportation, a state-sponsored old-age pension, guaranteed minimum income, free education, or a healthcare of the highest standards for all. The modern state socialists do not recognize that the more comprehensive the welfare state becomes, the more the beneficiaries themselves must pay for what they get.

The wealthy persons of the society will care for the poor if redistribution remains small and if the circle of the needy is well defined. This is the case with voluntary charity. Yet when the state expands into the welfare state, the beneficiaries of the social transfers must de facto assume the costs themselves for what they seem to get free from the state. The more the general population falls into the grip of the welfare state, the more diffuse the definition of need becomes and the larger the number of the contributors will grow. In the end, all pay more than they get.

If the redistribution in capitalism does not work, so some seem to ponder, only to impose full socialism will solve the problem of 'injustice'. In doing so, these socialists believe that they are good-hearted when they advocate socialism, yet they do not know that they speak in favor of an inhuman regime whose first victims would probably be they themselves.

While the socialism of the Soviet pattern is not the dominant ideology of our time, the anti-capitalist mentality is still virulent, and this ideology is all over in the media, the schools, and the universities. Like with their predecessors, the great error of the modern socialists is to believe that poverty originates from capitalism.

History has shown that socialism does exist as <u>tyranny</u>. With the choice for interventionism and socialism, economic stagnation comes while the decision for a free market economy leads to economic progress. Theory and history confirm that socialism is inseparable from stagnation, suppression, and poverty while capitalism is the more productive the freer it is.

A look at the experiences with the Communist rule makes the diagnosis unambiguous. Yet popular discontent runs against the capitalist economic order. There is a widespread illusion that one could have both the wealth of capitalism and the supposed socialist equality and justice.

The modern state has a structure that is very different from the original ideas of classical liberalism and in some respects, it is the opposite. Instead of having less state, liberal democracy comes with more intervention; instead of more individual liberty, the current system has extended its control over the individual. The majority voting system as it is currently in place leads to interventionism, and from there, socialism is only a step away. Democracy does not protect against folly or tyranny.

History does not have an inevitable path of development but there are economic laws. The decision for this or that version of the economic system is free, but the consequences are not free to choose. Freedom refers to the choice of institutions, not to their consequences.

In this sense, there is a power of ideas, and at the same time, there is the impotence of ideas in the face of facts. There are situations where, as the saying goes, that one cannot change the things anymore. Before the wrong decision was made, the path was open as the options laid on the table. A different choice could have evaded the problems that have surfaced now as a consequence of the wrong decision and the course of history would have gone in another direction.

The alternatives are clear. On the one hand, free capitalism as an economic order that brings personal liberty and overall prosperity, and, on the other hand, the socialist command economy, leading to poverty and suppression. The 21st century will belong to those nations that choose the path to free capitalism.

BEYOND THE STATE AND POLITICS

Demarchy — also called sortition — is a form of governance that selects the representatives of the people as a random sample from a pool of candidates. Such a governance by selecting the people's representatives by lottery instead of elections can look back on a venerable history.
For Aristotle, to select the people's political representatives by lot instead of voting distinguishes the democracy from oligarchical rule: 'So it is ... democratic to occupy the offices by lot, and for the oligarchy by vote' (Aristotle, *Politics*, IV, 9, 1294b 7-9). Likewise, for Montesquieu in "The Spirit of the Laws," the lottery procedure corresponds to "the nature of democracy."
In the ancient Greek polis, for the "Great Council of the 500," as well as for judges and for some state officials, selection took place by the lot — as it is still partly the case in Switzerland.
In the Republic of Venice, the selection procedure for the government and its members used the lottery in many ways. Until the 17th century, England also practiced the lottery system. Today, modern technology offers the possibility to apply random selection procedures to large populations.
The following advantages of demarchy are evident:

- High degree of popular legitimacy
- Independence of the representatives
- Absence of corruption
- No political parties
- Representation by normal people instead by political power seekers
- Elimination of the costs of the election campaigns
- Reduction of the overall cost of the political apparatus
- Comprehensible laws
- End of the inflation of laws, rules, and regulations
- Minimization of the state (less government spending, lower taxes).

Critics of demarchy claim that a parliament, whose members are selected by chance, has less expertise than an elected parliament, and that this would increase the power of the bureaucracy. The truth, however, is that the specific knowledge that is now present in the assemblies, exists in knowing how to gain and to exert power, and non-political competence is missing. Even more so, the current system of party politics has led to a huge bureaucracy and a massive build-up of the power of the state apparatus. The political parties and the bureaucracy cooperate to maximize their power which they achieve by having more state, not less.

The libertarian revolution is a soft revolution without violence. This is and will make the big difference between the anarcho-capitalist order and all other forms of governance. For the libertarian revolution to succeed, one must not '"take power," but conquer the public opinion by persuasion.

With the support of the public to change the structure of the party democracy, the first step would be to complement the present system with an additional chamber. In this chamber — a kind of "Senate" or "Upper House" — members chosen by lot would possess veto rights over the decisions taken by the parliament (Congress) and government (Presidency) including the judiciary (Supreme Court). Such a "fourth power" is the "voice of the people.". Although it is not yet a government and not yet the lawgiver, the 'Senate' composed by members chosen by lot has the right to stop the encroachments of government and of the state bureaucracy because of the veto power it holds.

The next step would be to create a "General Assembly" to serve as the prime law-giving body. The Assembly must be large enough to represent the people. For that purpose, it must comprise persons who are selected randomly among the constituency. Establishing the General Assembly requires a reform of the election laws. In order to achieve this, the libertarians must get a majority in the existing parliament (Congress). The final step in the reform of the state structure is to add a supervisory body and an executive branch of the Assembly.

The resulting institutional setting would include three organs: The General Assembly as the representative of the people and the prime law-giver, the Supervisory Body as a special committee to supervise the Executive branch that manages the current affairs of the polity. The last step would be the outsourcing of the governmental function to a private government management company under the supervision of the General Assembly.

FIGURES AND TABLES

I. The curse of socialism
- State murders by socialist regimes
- Democides by the Soviet regime
- Basic organizational structure of the planned economy
- Command chain an execution feedback
- Production direction and value determination
- Design effects of socialism
- Capitalist crisis cycle
- Summary

II. The fiasco of interventionism
- Varieties of state capitalism
- Rational irrationality
- Legacy of interventionism
- Economic growth of the United State since 1950
- GDP annual growth - official and shadow statistics
- Free market price equilibrium
- Price ceiling
- Price floor
- Main areas of state intervention
- Types of unemployment
- Keynesian and classical models of unemployment
- Productivity rates of industrialized countries since 1975
- Wage policy and unemployment

III. Welfare: More costs than benefits
- Costs of medical care, 1997-2017
- Life expectancy and spending on healthcare
- College costs and general price index since 1980
- US Universities - Selectivity and income by subject areas
- Government spending in percent of gdp
- Government spending for social purposes
- Social issues
- Types of justice

IV. Perpetual fiscal and monetary crises
- US government debt, 1970-2017
- US government debt ratio, 1935-2017
- Public debt ratios of selected countries
- Determinants of the debt burden
- Stylized central bank balance sheet
- Stylized commercial bank balance sheet
- Stages of money creation
- Types of assets
- Monetary aggregates of the US Federal Reserve System

BIBLIOGRAPHICAL REFERENCES

Achen, Christopher H. and Larry M. Bartels: Democracy for Realists: Why Elections Do Not Produce Responsive Government (Princeton Studies in Political Behavior) Princeton University Press 2017

Antonopoulos, Andreas M.: The Internet of Money. Merkle Bloom LLC. 2016

Applebaum, Anne: Gulag. A History. Anchor Books. 2004

Applebaum, Anne: Red Famine: Stalin's War on the Ukraine. Doubleday. 2017

Ashford, Nigel and Stephen Davis (eds.): A Dictionary of Conservative and Libertarian Thought (Routledge Revivals). Routledge. 2012

Bagus, Philipp: In Defense of Deflation (Financial and Monetary Policy Studies). Springer 2014

Bagus, Phillipp and Andreas Marquart: Blind Robbery!: How the Fed, Banks and Government Steal Our Money. FinanzBuch Verlag. 2016

Baldwin, Richard: The Great Convergence: Information Technology and the New Globalization. Belknap Press. 2016

Banerjee, Abhijit, and Esther Duflo: Poor Economics: A Radical Rethinking of the Way to Fight Global Poverty. Public Affairs. 2012

Barnett, Anthony: The Athenian Option: Radical Reform for the House of Lords (Sortition and Public Policy Book 5). Imprint Academic. 2017

Barrat, James: Our Final Invention: Artificial Intelligence and the End of the Human Era. St Martin's Griffin. 2015

Belke, Ansgar and Thorsten Polleit: Monetary Economics in Globalised Financial Markets. Springer. 2009

Belloc, Hilaire: The Servile State. T. N. Foulis 1912

Benda, Julien: The Treason of the Intellectuals. Routledge. 2006

Benson, Bruce L: The Enterprise of Law: Justice Without the State. Independent Institute. 2011

Birner, Jack and Pierre Garrouste (eds): Markets, Information and Communication: Austrian Perspectives on the Internet Economy (Routledge Foundations of the Market Economy). Routledge. 2003

Block, Walter: Defending the Undefendable. Ludwig von Mises Institute. 2008

Block, Walter: The Privatization of Roads and Highways: Human and Economic Factors. CreateSpace Independent Publishing Platform. 2012

Block, Walter: Toward a Libertarian Society. Ludwig von Mises Institute. 2014

Boaz, David (ed.). The Libertarian Reader: Classic & Contemporary Writings from Lao-Tzu to Milton Friedman. Simon & Schuster 2015

Boaz, David: The Libertarian Mind. A Manifesto for Freedom. Simon & Schuster. 2015

Boehm-Bawerk, Eugen von: Karl Marx and the Close of His System: A Criticism (Classic Reprint). Forgotten Books. 2012

Boehm-Bawerk, Eugen von: Positive Theory of Capital. Ludwig von Mises Institute. 2007

Bostroum, Nick: Superintelligence: Paths, Dangers, Strategies. Oxford University Press 2016

Boetie, Etienne de la: The Politics of Obedience: The Discourse of Voluntary Servitude. With an Introduction by Murray Rothbard. Ludwig von Mises Insitute. 2015

Boettke, Peter J.: Living Economics: Yesterday, Today, and Tomorrow (Independent Studies in Political Economy). Independent Institute. 2012

Boettke, Peter J.: Calculation and Coordination: Essays on Socialism and Transitional Political Economy (Routledge Foundations of the Market Economy). Routledge 2001

Boettke, Peter J.: The Oxford Handbook of Austrian Economics (Oxford Handbooks). Oxford University Press. 2015

Boettker, Peter J.: The Political Economy of Soviet Socialism: the Formative Years, 1918-1928. 1990th Edition. Springer 1990

Boldrin, Michele and David K. Levine. Against Intellectual Monopoly. Cambridge University Press. 2010

Bourdieu, Pierre: On the State: Lectures at the College de France, 1989 - 1992. Polity 2015

Bouricius, Terry: (S)election: Sortition, the democratic alternative (Fomite Interrogations: A Series of Tracts for Our Time) (Volume 6). Fomite Publishers 2017

Boyes, William J.: Managerial Economics: Markets and the Firm (Upper Level Economics Titles). South-Western College Publications. 2011

Brafman, Ori and Rod A. Becksstrom: The Starfish and the Spider: The Unstoppable Power of Leaderless Organizations. **Portfolio. 2008**

Brafman, Ori and Rod A. Becksstrom: The Starfish and the Spider: The Unstoppable Power of Leaderless Organizations. **Portfolio. 2008**

Brackins, Daniel Alexander: Private Property, the Law, and the State. CreateSpace Independent Publishing Platform. 2017

Braun, Eduard: Finance behind the Veil of Money. CreateSpace Independent Publishing Platform. 2016

Brennan, Jason: Against Democracy. Princeton University Press. 2016

Brick, Howard: Transcending Capitalism: Visions of a New Society in Modern American Thought. Cornell University Press. 2016

Brynjolfsson, Eric and Andrew McAfee: The Second Machine Age: Work, Progress, and Prosperity in a Time of Brilliant Technologies. W. W. Norton & Company. 2016

Buchanan, James and Richard Wagner: Democracy in Deficit. The Legacy of Lord Keynes. Emerald Group Publishing. 1977

Burnheim, John: The Demarchy Manifesto. For Better Public Policy (Societas). Imprint Academic 2016

Burnheim, John: Is Democracy Possible? The Alternative to Electoral Politics. University of California Press. 1985

Burnheim, John: The Demarchy Manifesto: For Better Public Policy (Societas). Imprint Academic. 2016

Bylund, Per L.: The Problem of Production: A new theory of the firm. Routledge 2015

Cachanosky, Nicolas: Monetary Equilibrium and Nominal Income Targeting (Routledge International Studies in Money and Banking). Routledge. 2018

Caplan, Bryan: The Case against Education: Why the Education System Is a Waste of Time and Money. Princeton University Press. 2018

Caplan, Bryan: The Myth of the Rational Voter: Why Democracies Choose Bad Policies. Princeton University Press. 2008

Chafuen, Alejandro A.: Faith and Liberty: The Economic Thought of the Late Scholastics (Studies in Ethics and Economics). Lexington Books. 2003

Christinsen, Clayton M.: The Innovator's Dilemma: When New Technologies Cause Great Firms to Fail (Management of Innovation and Change). Harvard Business Review Press. 2016

Clark, Gregory: A Farewell to Alms: A Brief Economic History of the World (The Princeton Economic History of the Western World). Princeton University Press. 2009

Cogan, John F.: The High Cost of Good Intentions: A History of U.S. Federal Entitlement Programs. Princeton University Press. 2017

Conquest, Robert: The Great Terror: A Reassessment 40th anniversary Edition. Oxford University Press. 2007

Conquest, Robert: The Harvest of Sorrow: Soviet Collectivization and the Terror-Famine. Oxford University Press; Reprint edition. 1987

Cowen, Tyler and Alex Tabarrok: Modern Principles of Economics. Worth Publishers. 2014

Cowen, Tyler: Average Is Over: Powering America Beyond the Age of the Great Stagnation. Plume. 2014

Cowen, Tyler: The Great Stagnation: How America Ate All the Low-Hanging Fruit of Modern History, Got Sick, and Will (Eventually) Feel Better. Dutton 2011

Coyne, Christopher J. and Abigail R. Hall: Tyranny Comes Home: The Domestic Fate of U.S. Militarism. Stanford University Press. 2018

Cwick, Paul F.: An Investigation of Inverted Yield Curves and Economic Downturns. Ludwig von Mises Institute.

Dahlen, Michael: Ending Big Government: The Essential Case for Capitalism and Freedom. Mill City Press. 2016

Dalrymple, Theodore: Nothing but Wickedness: The Origins of the Decline of Our Culture. Gibson Square Books. 2018

Davidson, James Dale and William Rees-Mogg: The Sovereign Individual: Mastering the Transition to the Information Age. Touchstone. 1999

Delannoi, Gil and Oliver Dowlen (eds.): Sortition: Theory and Practice (Sortition and Public Policy). Imprint Academic. 2010

Deneen, Patrick J.: Why Liberalism Failed (Politics and Culture). Yale University Press. 2018

Diamandis, Peter H. and Steven Kotler: Abundance: The Future Is Better Than You Think. Free Press. Reprint edition. 2014

Di Iorio, Francesco: Cognitive Autonomy and Methodological Individualism: The Interpretative Foundations of Social Life (Studies in Applied Philosophy, Epistemology and Rational Ethics). Springer 2015

Dilorenzo Thomas J.: How Capitalism Saved America: The Untold History of Our Country, from the Pilgrims to the Present. Crown Forum. 2005
Dilorenzo, Thomas: The Problem with Socialism. **Regnery Publishing. 2016**

Doherty, Brian: Radicals for Capitalism: A Freewheeling History of the Modern American Libertarian Movement. Public Affairs. 2008

Dorn, James A. (ed.): Monetary Alternatives: Rethinking Government Fiat Money. Cato Institute 2017

Dorn, James A., Steve H. Hanke and Alan A. Sir Walters (eds.); The Revolution in Development Economics. Cato Institute. 1998

Dowlen, Oliver: The Political Potential of Sortition: A study of the random selection of citizens for public office (Sortition and Public Policy). Imprint Academic 2009

Drochon, Hugo: Nietzsche's Great Politics. Princeton University Press. 2016
Drucker, Peter: Innovation and Entrepreneurship. HarperBusiness. 2006

Easterbrook, Gregg: It's Better Than It Looks: Reasons for Optimism in an Age of Fear. PublicAffairs. 2018

Easterly, William R.: The Elusive Quest for Growth: Economists' Adventures and Misadventures in the Tropics. The MIT Press. 2002

Easterly, William: The White Man's Burden: Why the West's Efforts to Aid the Rest Have Done So Much Ill and So Little Good. Penguin. 2007

Easterly, William R.: The Tyranny of Experts: Economists, Dictators, and the Forgotten Rights of the Poor. Basic Books. 2015

Ebeling, Richard and Jacob G. Hornberger: The Failure of America's Foreign Wars. Future of Freedom Foundation. 1996

Ebeling, Richard M.: Monetary Central Planning and the State. The Future of Freedom Foundation. 2015

Emerson, Ralph Waldo: The Essential Writings of Ralph Waldo Emerson (Modern Library Classics). Modern Library. 2000

Eire, N. N. Carlos: Reformations: The Early Modern World, 1450-1650. Yale University Press. 2016

Eucken, Walter: The Foundations of Economics: History and Theory in the Analysis of Economic Reality. Springer. 2011

Eusepi, Guiseppe and Richard E. Wagner: Public Debt: An Illusion of Democratic Political Economy (New Thinking in Political Economy series). Edward Elgar Publications. 2017

Erhard, Ludwig: Prosperity Through Competition. Praeger. 1958

Ertel, Wolfgang: Introduction to Artificial Intelligence (Undergraduate Topics in Computer Science). Springer 2018

Evans, Anthony J.: Markets for Managers: A Managerial Economics Primer (The Wiley Finance Series). Wiley. 2014

Evans, Michelle and Augusto Zimmermann(eds.): Global Perspectives on Subsidiarity (Ius Gentium: Comparative Perspectives on Law and Justice). Springer 2014

Evans, Stanton M.: Stalin's Secret Agents: The Subversion of Roosevelt's Government. Threshold Editions. 2013

Ebeling, Richard: Austrian Economics and Public Policy. Restoring Freedom and Prosperity. The Future of Freedom Foundation. 2016

Ferguson, Niall: The Square and the Tower: Networks and Power, from the Freemasons to Facebook. Penguin Press. 2018

Ferguson, Niall: Civilization: The West and the Rest. Penguin Books. 2012
Fareed, Zakaria: The Future of Freedom: Illiberal Democracy at Home and Abroad (Revised Edition). W. W. Norton & Company. 2007

Feyerabend, Paul: Against Method. Verso. 2010

Folsom, Burton W.: The Myth of the Robber Barons: A New Look at the Rise of Big Business in America. Young America Foundation. 1991

Ford, Martin: The Rise of the Robots: Technology and the Threat of a Jobless Future. Basic Book. Reprint edition. 2015

Foss, Nikolai J. and Peter Klein (eds.): Entrepreneurship and the Firm: Austrian Perspectives on Economic Organization. Edward Elgar Publishing. 2002

Frank, Malcolm, Paul Roehrig, Ben Pring: What To Do When Machines Do Everything: How to Get Ahead in a World of AI, Algorithms, Bots, and Big Data. Wiley 2017

Friedman, David D.: The Machinery of Freedom: Guide to Radical Capitalism. CreateSpace Independent Publishing Platform; 3rd edition. 2015

Friedman, Milton and Anna Jacobson Schwartz: A Monetary History of the United States, 1867-1960. Princeton University Press. 1971

Friedman, Milton: Capitalism and Freedom. Fortieth Anniversary Edition. University of Chicago Press. 2002

Fukuyama, Francis: The Origins of Political Order: From Prehuman Times to the French Revolution. Farrar, Straus and Giroux. 2012

Garrison, Roger: Time and Money: The Macroeconomics of Capital Structure (Routledge Foundations of the Market Economy) New Edition. Routledge 2007

Gatto, John Taylor: The Underground History of American Education, Volume I: An Intimate Investigation Into the Prison of Modern Schooling. Valor Academy 2017

Guerin, Daniel (ed.): No Gods No Masters: An Anthology of Anarchism. AK Press 2005

Giddens, Anthony: The Third Way: The Renewal of Social Democracy. Polity Press. 1999

Giddens, Anthony: Capitalism and Modern Social Theory: An Analysis of the Writings of Marx, Durkheim and Max Weber. Cambridge University Press. 1973

Goodwin, Barbara: Justice by Lottery (Sortition and Public Policy). Imprint Academic 2005

Gordon, Robert J. : The Rise and Fall of American Growth: The U.S. Standard of Living since the Civil War (The Princeton Economic History of the Western World). Princeton University Press 2017

Gordon, David: An Austro-Libertarian View: Current Affairs, Foreign Policy, American History, European History (Essays by David Gordon). 3 vols. The Ludwig von Mises Institute. 2017

Granovetter, Marc: Society and Economy: Framework and Principles. Belknap Press: An Imprint of Harvard University Press. 2017

Grant, James: The Forgotten Depression: 1921: The Crash That Cured Itself. Simon & Schuster. 2014

Halberstam, Davin: The Best and the Brightest. Modern Library. 2002

Harford, Tim: Fifty Inventions that Shaped the Modern Economy. Riverhead Books. 2017

Harris, Fred and Alan Curtis (eds.): Healing Our Divided Society: Investing in America Fifty Years after the Kerner Report. Temple University Press. 2018

Harwood Economics Review. Socialism Issue. American Institute for Economic Research. Fall 2018

Haskel, Jonathan and Stian Westlake: Capitalism without Capital: The Rise of the Intangible. Princeton University Press. 2017

Hathaway, Oona A. and Scott J. Shapiro: The Internationalists: How a Radical Plan to Outlaw War Remade the World. Simon & Schuster. 2017

Hayek, Friedrich A. von: Individualism and Economic Order. University of Chicago Press. 1996
Hayek, Friedrich A. von: The Constitution of Liberty: The Definitive Edition (The Collected Works of F. A. Hayek). University of Chicago Press. 2011

Hayek, Friedrich A. von: The Road to Serfdom: Text and Documents -The Definitive Edition (The Collected Works of F. A. Hayek, Volume 2). University of Chicago Press. 2007

Hayek, Friedrich A.: Denationalisation of Money. The Argument Refined. CreateSpace Independent Publishing Platform. 2014

Hazlitt, Henry: Economics in One Lesson: The Shortest and Surest Way to Understand Basic Economics. Crown Business. 1988

Hazlitt, Henry: The Failure of the New Economics. Martino Fine Books. 2016

Heidegger, Martin: The Question Concerning Technology, and Other Essays (Harper Perennial Modern Thought). Harper Perennial Modern Classics; Reissue edition. 2013

Hennig, Brett: The End of Politicians: Time for a Real Democracy. Unbound Digital. 2017

Herbener, Jeffrey M. : Pure Time-Preference Theory of Interest. Ludwig von Mises Institute. 2011

Heyne, Paul L., Peter J. Boettke, and David L. Prychito: The Economic Way of Thinking. Pearson Series in Economics. 2013

Hicks, Stephen, R. C.: Explaining Postmodernism: Skepticism and Socialism from Rousseau to Foucault (Expanded Edition). Ockham's Razor Publishers. 2011

Higgs, Robert: Against Leviathan: Government Power and a Free Society (Independent Studies in Political Economy). Independent Institute. 2004

Higgs, Robert: Crisis and Leviathan: Critical Episodes in the Growth of American Government, 25th Anniversary Edition (Independent Studies in Political Economy). Independent Institute; Anniversary edition. 2013

Higgs, Robert: Depression, War, and Cold War: Studies in Political Economy. Oxford University Press. 2006

Higgs, Robert: Taking a Stand: Reflections on Life, Liberty, and the Economy. Independent Institute. 2015

Hirschman, Albert O.: The Passions and the Interests. Political Arguments before its Triumph (Princeton Classics). Princeton University. 2013

Hirschmann, Albert O.: Exit, Voice, and Loyalty: Responses to Decline in Firms, Organizations, and States. Harvard University Press 1970

Holcombe, Randall G.: Advanced Introduction to Public Choice (Elgar Advanced Introductions series). Edward Elgar Publishers. 2016

Holcombe, Randall G.: Advanced Introduction to the Austrian School of Economics (Elgar Advanced Introductions series). Edgar Elgar Publishers. 2014

Holcombe, Randall G.: Producing Prosperity: An Inquiry into the Operation of the Market Process (Routledge Foundations of the Market Economy). Routledge 2015

Holcombe, Randall G.: Entrepreneurship and Economic Progress (Routledge Foundations of the Market Economy). Routledge 2006

Hoppe, Hans-Hermann: A Short History of Man: Progress and Decline. Ludwig von Mises Institute 2015

Hoppe, Hans-Hermann: A Theory of Socialism and Capitalism. Ludwig von Mises Institute. 2003

Hoppe, Hans-Hermann: Democracy. The God that Failed: Economics and Politics of Monarchy, Democracy and Natural Order (Perspectives on Democratic Practice. Routledge. 2001

Hoppe, Hans-Hermann: The Economics and Ethics of Private Property: Studies in Political Economy and Philosophy, 2nd Edition. Ludwig von Mises Institute. 2010

Hoppe, Hans-Herman: The Myth of National Defense: Essays on the Theory and History of Security Production. Ludwig von Mises Institute. 2003

Horwitz, Steve: Hayek's Modern Family: Classical Liberalism and the Evolution of Social Institutions. Palgrave Macmillan. 2015

Howden, David and Joseph T. Salerno (eds.): The Fed at One Hundred: A Critical View on the Federal Reserve System. Springer. 2014

Huebert, Jacob H.: Libertarianism Today. Praeger 2010

Huerta de Soto, Jesus: Money, Bank Credit, and Economic Cycles. Ludwig von Mises Institute. 2012

Hülsmann, Jörg Guido and Stephan Kinsella (eds.): Property, Freedom, and Society: Essays in Honor of Hans-Hermann Hoppe (LvMI). Ludwig von Mises Institute 2011

Hülsmann, Jörg Guido: The Ethics of Money Production. Ludwig von Mises Institute. 2008

Humboldt, Wilhelm von: The Sphere and Duties of Government (The Limits of State Action). Martino Fine Books. 2014

Illich, Ivan: Deschooling Society (Open Forum S). Marion Boyars Publishers Ltd; New edition edition. 2000

Illich, Ivan: Limits to Medicine: Medical Nemesis, the Expropriation of Health. Marion Boyars Publishers Ltd; Revised ed. Edition. 2000

Infantino, Lorenzo: Individualism in Modern Thought: From Adam Smith to Hayek (Routledge Studies in Social and Political Thought). Routledge 2014

Irwin, Douglas A.: Against the Tide. An Intellectual History of Free Trade. Princeton University Press. 1996

Joshi, Vijay: India's Long Road: The Search for Prosperity. Oxford University Press. 2017

Juma, Calestous: Innovation and Its Enemies: Why People Resist New Technologies. Oxford University Press. 2016

Kant, Imanuel and H.S. Reiss (ed). Kant: Political Writings (Cambridge Texts in the History of Political Thought). Cambridge University Press. 1991

Kealey, Terence: The Case Against Public Science. Cato Unbound. August 2013

Kealey, Terence: The Economic Laws of Scientific Research. Palgrave Macmillan. 1996

Kengor, Paul: The Politically Incorrect Guide to Communism (The Politically Incorrect Guides). Regnery Publishing 2017

Kenny, Charles: Getting Better: Why Global Development Is Succeeding - And How We Can Improve the World Even More. Basic Books. 2012

Keynes, John Maynard: The General Theory of Employment, Interest and Money: With the Economic Consequences of the Peace (Classics of World Literature). Wordworth Editions 2017

Kinsella, Stephan: Against Intellectual Property. Ludwig von Mises Institute. 2015

Kirzner, Israel: Competition and Entrepreneurship (The Collected Works of Israel M. Kirzner). Liberty Fund. 2013

Knight, Frank: Risk, Uncertainty and Profit. Martino Fine Books. 2014

Kocka, Jürgen: Capitalism. A Short History. Princeton University Press. 2017

Kroeber, Arthur A.: China's Economy: What Everyone Needs to Know. Oxford University Press. 2016

Kuehnelt-Leddihn: Eric Ritter von: Liberty or Equality: The Challenge of Our Times. The Ludwig von Mises Institute. 2014

Kuehnelt-Leddihn: Eric Ritter von: Menace of the Herd or Procrustes at Large. Ludwig von Mises Institute. 2012

Kurer, Oskar: John Stuart Mill (Routledge Revivals): The Politics of Progress. Routledge 2018
Kurer, Oskar: The Political Foundations of Development Policies. UPA Publishers 1996

Kurlansky, Mark: Nonviolence: The History of a Dangerous Idea (Modern Library Chronicles). Modern Library 2008

Kurzweil, Ray: The Singularity Is Near: When Humans Transcend Biology. Penguin Books. 2006

Lavoie, Don: Rivalry and Central Planning. The Socialist Calculation Debate Reconsidered (Advanced Studies in Political Economy). Mercatus Center at George Mason University. 2015

Leeson, Peter: Anarchy Unbound: Why Self-Governance Works Better Than You Think (Cambridge Studies in Economics, Choice, and Society). Cambridge University Press. 2014

Leonard, Thomas C.: Illiberal Reformers: Race, Eugenics, and American Economics in the Progressive Era. Princeton University Press. 2017

Legutko, Ryszard: The Demon in Democracy: Totalitarian Temptations in Free Societies. Encounter Books. 2016

Lenin, Vladimir Ilich: State and Revolution. Martino Fine Books. 2011

Leoni, Bruno: Freedom and the Law. Liberty Fund. 1991

Lerch, Hubert: An Introduction to Political Philosophy. CreateSpace Independent Publishing Platform. 2011

Levin, Mark R.: Rediscovering Americanism: And the Tyranny of Progressivism. Threshold Editions. 2017

Levitsky, Steven and Daniel Zieblatt: How Democracies Die. Crown 2018

Lewis, Hunter: Economics in Three Lessons and One Hundred Economics Laws: Two Works in One Volume. Axios Press. 2017

Lewis, Hunter: Where Keynes Went Wrong: And Why World Governments Keep Creating Inflation, Bubbles, and Busts. Axios Press. 2009

Lilla, Mark: The Once and Future Liberal: After Identity Politics. Harper. 2017

Lindsay, Brink: The Age of Abundance: How Prosperity Transformed America's Politics and Culture. Harper Business Reprint edition. 2008

Lingle, Christopher: The Rise and Decline of the Asian Century: False Starts on the Path to the Global Millennium. Bookworld Services. 1998

Lingle, Christopher: The Rise and Decline of the Asian Century: False Starts on the Path to the Global Millennium. Bookworld Services. 1998

Machaj, Mateusz: Money, Interest, and the Structure of Production: Resolving Some Puzzles in the Theory of Capital (Capitalist Thought: Studies in Philosophy, Politics, and Economics). Lexington Books. 2017

Mallaby, Sebastian: The Man Who Knew: The Life and Times of Alan Greenspan. Penguin Books. 2017

Maltsev, Yuri: Requiem for Marx. CreateSpace Independent Publishing Platform. 1993

Maltsev, Yuri: Mass Murder and Public Slavery: The Soviet Experience. The Independent Review 2017

Mandeville, Bernard: The Fable of the Bees and Other Writings (Hackett Classics). Hacket Publishing Company. 1997

Marx, Karl: Das Kapital: A Critique of Political Economy. CreateSpace Independent Publishing Platform. 2011

Marx, Karl and Friedrich Engels: The Communist Manifesto. International Publishers Co; New edition. 2014

McCaffrey, Matthew: The Economic Theory of Costs: Foundations and New Directions (Routledge Frontiers of Political Economy). Routledge 2017

McCloskey, Deirdre: The Bourgeois Virtues: Ethics for an Age of Commerce. University of Chicago Press. 2007

McGroarty, Emmett, Jane Robbins, and Erin Tuttle: Deconstructing the Administrative State. Liberty Hill Publishing. 2017

McLuhan, Marshall: The Gutenberg Galaxy. University of Toronto Press, Scholarly Publishing Division. 2011

Menger, Carl: Principles of Economics. CreateSpace Independent Publishing Platform. 2007

Mencken, H. L.: Notes on Democracy. CreateSpace Independent Publishing Platform. 2013

Mesquita, Bruce Bueno de and Alistair Smith: The Dictator's Handbook: Why Bad Behavior is Almost Always Good Politics. PublicAffairs. 2012

Mierzejewski, Alfred C.: Ludwig Erhard: A Biography. University of North Carolina Press. 2014

Mill, John Stuart: On Liberty, Utilitarianism and Other Essays (Oxford World's Classics). Cambridge University Press. 2015

Miller, Tom: China's Asian Dream: Empire Building along the New Silk Road. Zed Books. 2017

Mises, Ludwig von: Human Action. The Scholar's Edition. Ludwig von Mises Institute. 2010

Mises, Ludwig von: Liberalism. Liberty Fund. 2005

Mises, Ludwig von: Economic Calculation in the Socialist Commonwealth. Ludwig von Mises Institute. 2012

Mises, Ludwig von: Interventionism: An Economic Analysis (Lib Works Ludwig Von Mises PB). Liberty Fund. 2011

Mokyr, Joel: A Culture of Growth: The Origins of the Modern Economy (Graz Schumpeter Lectures). Princeton University Press 2016

Mokyr, Joel: Gift of Athena: Historical Origins of the Knowledge Economy. Princeton University Press 2014

Mokyr, Joel: The Lever of Riches: Technological Creativity and Economic Progress. Oxford University Press. 1992

Molyneux, Stefan: Practical Anarchy. The Freedom of the Future. CreateSpace Independent Publishing Platform. 2017

Mueller, Antony P.: Bubble or New Era? Monetary Aspects of the New Economy. In: Birner, Jack and Pierre Garrouste (eds): Markets, Information and Communication: Austrian Perspectives on the Internet Economy (Routledge Foundations of the Market Economy). Routledge. 2003, pp. 249-261

Muller, Jerry Z.: The Tyranny of Metrics. Princeton University Press. 2018

Muller, Jerry Z.: The Mind and the Market: Capitalism in Western Thought. Anchor. 2003

Murphy, Robert: The Politically Incorrect Guide to the Great Depression and the New Deal (The Politically Incorrect Guides). Regnery Publishing. 2009

Murphy, Robert: Choice: Cooperation, Enterprise, and Human Action. Independent Institute. 2015

Molinari, Gustave de: The Production of Security. Edited by Richard Ebeling with an Introduction by Murray Rothbard. Create Space. 2009

Murray, Charles: In Our Hands: A Plan to Replace the Welfare State. AEI Press. 2016

Murray, Charles: By the People: Rebuilding Liberty Without Permission. Crown Forum. 2015

Murray, Charles: Losing Ground: American Social Policy, 1950-1980. Basic Books. 2015

Nietzsche, Friedrich: The Will to Power. Independently published. 2017

Niskanen, William A.: Reaganomics: An Insider's Account of the Policies and the People. Oxford University Press. 1988

Norberg, Johan: Ten Reasons to Look Forward to the Future. Oneworld Publication. 2017

North, Douglas C. and Robert Paul Thomas: The Rise of the Western World: A New Economic History. Cambridge University Press. 1976

North, Douglass C.: Institutions, Institutional Change and Economic Performance (Political Economy of Institutions and Decisions) Cambridge University Press. 1990

North, Gary: Mises on Money. Ludwig von Mises Institute. 2012

Novak, Michael and Paul Adams: Social Justice Isn't What You Think It Is. Encounter Books. 2015

Nozick, Robert: Anarchy, State, and Utopia. Basic Books Reprint. 2013

O'Driscoll, Gerald P. and Maria Rizzo: The Economics of Time and Ignorance. Routledge Foundations of the Market Economy. Routledge 1996

OECD (Organization for Economic Cooperation and Development: The Sources of Economic Growth in OECD Countries. OECD 2003

Oliver, Michael J.: The New Libertarianism: Anarcho-Capitalism. CreateSpace. 2013

Olson, Mancur: The Logic of Collective Action. Public Goods and the Theory of Groups. Second printing with new preface and appendix (Harvard Economic Studies). Harvard University Press. 1971

Oppenheimer, Franz: The State: Its History and Development Viewed Sociologically. (Classic Reprint). Forgotten Books. 2012

O'Rourke, P. J.: Parliament of Whores: A Lone Humorist Attempts to Explain the Entire U.S. Government. Grove Press. 2003

O'Rourke, P. J.: Eat the Rich: A Treatise on Economics. Atlantic Monthly Press. 1999

Ortega y Gasset, José: The Revolt of the Masses. W. W. Norten & Company. 1994

Ostrom, Elinor: Governing the Commons: The Evolution of Institutions for Collective Action (Canto Classics). Cambridge University Press; Reissue edition. 2015

Ostrowski, James: Progressivism: A Primer on the Idea Destroying America. Cazenovia Books. 2014

Palmer, Tom: Realizing Freedom: Libertarian Theory, History, and Practice. Cato Institute. 2014

Palmer, Tom G, Virginia Prostel, Brink Lindsey, and Tyler Cowen: Libertarianism. Past and Prospects (Cato Unbound Book 32007). Cato Institute. 2007

Parijs, Philippe Van and Yannick Vanderborght: Basic Income: A Radical Proposal for a Free Society and a Sane Economy. Harvard University Press. 2017

Paul, Ron: End the Fed. Grand Central Publishing. 2010

Paul, Ron: Revolution. A Manifesto. Grand Central Publishing. 2009

Pesek, William: Japanization: What the World Can Learn from Japan's Lost Decades. Wiley 2014

Pilling, David: The Growth Delusion: Wealth, Poverty, and the Well-Being of Nations. Tim Duggan Books. 2018

Pinker, Steven: Enlightenment Now: The Case for Reason, Science, Humanism, and Progress. Viking 2018

Pinker, Steven: The Better Angels of Our Nature: Why Violence Has Declined. Penguin Books. 2012

Postrel, Virginia: The Future and Its Enemies: The Growing Conflict Over Creativity, Enterprise. Free Press. 2011

Powell, Benjamin: Out of Poverty: Sweatshops in the Global Economy (Cambridge Studies in Economics, Choice, and Society). Cambridge University Press. 2014

Powell, Jim: FDR's Folly: How Roosevelt and His New Deal Prolonged the Great Depression. Crown Forum. 2004

Powell, James and Paul Johnson: The Triumph of Liberty: A 2,000 Year History Told Through the Lives of Freedom's Greatest Champions. Free Press. 2000

Qui, Insula: Capitalism Works. Independently published. 2018

Rachels, Chase and Christopher Chase Rachels: A Spontaneous Order: The Capitalist Case for a Stateless Society. CreateSpace Independent Publishing Platform. 2015

Raico, Ralph: Classical Liberalism and the Austrian School. CreateSpace Independent Publishing Platform. 2012

Raico, Ralph: Great Wars and Great Leaders: A Libertarian Rebuttal. Ludwig von Mises Institute. 2015

Ratner-Rosenhagen, Jennifer: American Nietzsche: A History of an Icon and His Ideas. University of Chicago Press; Reprint edition. 2012

Rawls, John: Justice as Fairness: A Restatement. Belknap Press: An Imprint of Harvard University Press. 2001

Rand, Ayn: Capitalism. The Unknown Ideal. Signet; Reissue edition. 1986

Reed, Lawrence R.: Great Myth of the Great Depression. Foundation for Economic Education. 2015

Reisman, George: Capitalism. A Treatise on Economics. TJS Books 1996

Reisman, George: The Government Against the Economy. Jameson Books. 1985

Reybrouck, David van: Against Elections. The Case for Democracy. Random House U.K. 2017

Reynolds, Morgan O.: Making America Poorer: The Cost of Labor Law. Cato Institute. 1987

Richman, Sheldon: America's Counter-Revolution: The Constitution Revisited. Grifien & Lash. 2016

Ridley, Matt: The Rational Optimist: How Prosperity Evolves. Harper Perennial. 2011

Rifkin, Jeremy: The Zero Marginal Cost Society: The Internet of Things, the Collaborative Commons, and the Eclipse of Capitalism. St. Martin's Griffin; Reprint edition. 2015

Ritenour, Shawn (ed.): The Mises Reader Unabridged. Ludwig von Mises Institute. 2016

Roberts, Paul Craig: The Tyranny of Good Intentions: How Prosecutors and Law Enforcement Are Trampling the Constitution in the Name of Justice. Crown. 2008

Rockwell, Llewellyn, H. Jr.: Against the State. An Anarcho-Capitalist Manifesto. Rockwell Communication. 2014

Rosenberg, Nathan and L. E. Birdzell: How the West Grew Rich: The Economic Transformation Of The Industrial World. Basic Books. 1987

Rosling, Hans, Anna Rosling Rönnlund, Ola Rosling: Factfulness: Ten Reasons We're Wrong About the World--and Why Things Are Better Than You Think. Flatiron Books 2018

Rothbard, Murray N.: Anatomy of the State. Bhpublishing. 2014

Rothbard, Murray N.: For a New Liberty. The Libertarian Manifesto. CreateSpace Independent Publishing Platform. 2006

Rothbard, Murray N.: What Has Government Done to Our Money? Ludwig von Mises Institute. 2015

Rothbard, Murray N.: Man, Economy, and State with Power and Market, Scholar's Edition. Ludwig von Mises Institute. 2011

Rothbard, Murray N.: America's Great Depression. Ludwig von Mises Institute. 2000

Rummel, Rudy J.: Death by Government: Genocide and Mass Murder Since 1900. Routledge 1997

Rummel, Rudy J.: The Blue Book of Freedom: Ending Famine, Poverty, Democide, and War. Cumberland House Publishing. 2007

Salerno, Joseph T.: Money: Sound and Unsound. Ludwig von Mises Institute. 2015

Say, Jean-Baptiste: A Treatise on Political Economy: Or the Production, Distribution and Consumption of Wealth. CreateSpace Independent Publishing Platform. 2013

Schiff, Peter: How an Economy Grows and Why It Crashes. Wiley. 2010

Schmitt, Carl: The Leviathan in the State Theory of Thomas Hobbes: Meaning and Failure of a Political Symbol (Heritage of Sociology). University of Chicago Press Ed Edition. 2008

Schmitt, Carl: The Concept of the Political: Expanded Edition Enlarged Edition with a Commentary by Leo Strauss. The University of Chicago Press. 2007

Schoolland, Ken: The Adventures of Jonathan Gullible. A Free Market Odyssey. Liberty Publishing. 2011

Schumpeter, Joseph A.: Business Cycles: A Theoretical, Historical, and Statistical Analysis of the Capitalist Process (2 Vols.). Martino Fine Books. 2017

Schumpeter, Joseph A.: Can Capitalism Survive?: Creative Destruction and the Future of the Global Economy. Harper Perennial Modern Classics. 2009

Schumpeter, Joseph A.: Capitalism, Socialism, and Democracy: Third Edition. Harper Perennial Modern Classics. 2008

Schumpeter, Joseph A.: Essays: On Entrepreneurs, Innovations, Business Cycles and the Evolution of Capitalism. Routledge 1989

Schumpeter, Joseph A.: Theory of Economic Development (Social Science Classics Series). Routledge 1981

Schwab, Klaus and Nicholas Davis, Satya Nadella: Shaping the Fourth Industrial Revolution. World Economic Forum. 2018

Scruton, Roger: Fools, Frauds and Firebrands: Thinkers of the New Left. Bloomsbury Continuum. 2017

Selgin, George: Financial Stability without Central Banks. London Publishing Partnership. 2018

Selgin, George: Money: Free and Unfree. Cato Institute. 2017

Selgin, George: Less Than Zero. The Case for a Falling Price Level in a Growing Economy. CreateSpace Independent Publishing Platform. 2014

Selgin, George: The Theory of Free Banking. Rowman & Littlefield Publisher. 1988

Sen, Amartya: Development as Freedom. Anchor. 2000

Sévillia, Jean: Le terrorisme intellectuel (French Edition). Tempus Perrain. 2017

Shaffer, Butler: Boundaries of Order: Private Property as a Social System. CreateSpace Independent Publishing Platform. 2009

Shaffer, Buttler: The Wizards of Ozymandias: Reflections on the Decline and Fall. CreateSpace Independent Publishing Platform. 2012

Shlae, Amity: The Forgotten Man: A New History of the Great Depression **Harper Perennial. 2008**

Simon, Julian Lincoln: The Ultimate Resource 2. **Princeton University Press. 1998**

Sintomer, Yves: Das demokratische Experiment: Geschichte des Losverfahrens in der Politik von Athen bis heute (German Edition). Springer 2016

Smiley, Gene: Rethinking the Great Depression (American Ways). Ivan R. Dee Publisher. 2003

Smith, Adam: The Theory of Moral Sentiments. Digireads.com. 2010

Smith, Adam: The Wealth of Nations (Bantam Classics). Bantam Classics; Annotated edition. 2003

Snyder, Timothy: On Tyranny: Twenty Lessons from the Twentieth Century. Tim Duggan Books. 2017

Sombart, Werner: The Quintessence Of Capitalism: A Study Of The History And Psychology Of The Modern Business Man. Scholar Select. Andesite Press. 2017

Solzhenitsyn, Aleksandr: The Gulag Archipelago. The Harvill Press. 2003

Soto, Hernando de: The Mystery of Capital: Why Capitalism Triumphs in the West and Fails Everywhere Else. Basic Books. 2003

Sowell, Thomas: Basic Economics. Basic Books. 2014

Sowell, Thomas: Economic Facts and Fallacies. Basic Books. 2011

Sowell, Thomas: The Quest for Cosmic Justice. Free Press 2002

Spencer, Herbert: Social Statics: Or, The Conditions Essential to Human Happiness Specified and the First of them Developed. Nabu Press. 2011

Srinivasa, Bhu: Americana: A 400-Year History of American Capitalism. Penguin Press. 2017

Steil, Ben: The Marshall Plan: Dawn of the Cold War. Simon & Schuster. 2018

Steil, Ben: The Battle of Bretton Woods: John Maynard Keynes, Harry Dexter White, and the Making of a New World Order (Council on Foreign Relations Books). Princeton University Press. 2014

Stirner, Max: The Ego and His Own: The Case of the Individual Against Authority (Dover Books on Western Philosophy). Dover Publications. 2005

Stone, Peter: Lotteries in Public Life: A Reader (Sortition and Public Policy). Imprint Academic. 2012

Stringham, Edward Peter: Private Governance: Creating Order in Economic and Social Life. Oxford University Press. 2015

Susskind, Richard and Daniel Susskind: The Future of the Professions: How Technology Will Transform the Work of Human Experts. Oxford University Press. Reprint edition. 2017

Suvorov, Viktor: Icebreaker. Who Started the Second World War? PL UK Publishing. 2012

Taleb, Nassim Nicholas: Skin in the Game: Hidden Asymmetries in Daily Life. Random House 2018

Taylor, Frederick: The Downfall of Money: Germany's Hyperinflation and the Destruction of the Middle Class. Bloomsbury Press. 2015

Taylor, Mark Zachary: The Politics of Innovation: Why Some Countries Are Better Than Others at Science and Technology. Oxford University Press. 2016

Thiel, Peter: Zero to One: Notes on Startups, or How to Build the Future. Currency Publishers. 2014

Thornton, Mark: The Bastiat Collection. Ludwig von Mises Institute. 2017

Thornton, Mark: The Economics of Prohibition. Ludwig von Mises Institute. 2014

Tilly, Charles: Coercion, Capital and European States, A.D. 990 - 1992. Wiley-Blackwell. 1992

Tirole, Jean: Economics for the Common Good. Princeton University Press. 2017

Tooley, Hunt: The Great War: Western Front and Home Front. Palgrave 2015

Tucker, Jeffrey: A Beautiful Anarchy: How to Create Your Own Civilization in the Digital Age. Laissez Faire Books. 2012

Vance, Laurence M.: War, Empire, and the Military: Essays on the Follies of War and U.S. Foreign Policy. Vance Publications. 2014

Vedder, Richard: Going Broke By Degree: Why College Cost. AEI Press. 2004

Veryser, Harry C.: It Didn't Have to Be This Way: Why Boom and Bust Is Unnecessary—and How the Austrian School of Economics Breaks the Cycle (Culture of Enterprise). ISI Books. 2013

Volcker, Paul and Toyoo Gyohten. Changing Fortunes. Crown. 1992

Walsh, Michael: The Devil's Pleasure Palace: The Cult of Critical Theory and the Subversion of the West. Encounter Books. 2017

White, Lawrence: The Clash of Economic Ideas: The Great Policy Debates and Experiments of the Last Hundred Years. Cambridge University Press. 2012

White, Lawrence: The Theory of Monetary Institutions. Wiley-Blackwell. 1999

White, Lawrence: Competition and Currency: Essays on Free Banking and Money. New York University Press. 1992

Wisniewski, Jakub: The Economics of Law, Order, and Action: The Logic of Public Goods (Routledge Advances in Heterodox Economics). Routledge. 2018

Williams, Walter E.: American Contempt for Liberty (Hoover Institution Press Publication). Hoover Institution Press 2015

Williams, Walter E.: Race & Economics: How Much Can Be Blamed on Discrimination?. Hoover Institution Press. 2011

Wolfram, Gary: A Capitalist Manifesto: Understanding The Market Economy And Defending Liberty. Dunlap Goddard. 2013

Woods, Thomas E.: Meltdown: A Free-Market Look at Why the Stock Market Collapsed, the Economy Tanked, and Government Bailouts Will Make Things Worse. Regnery 2009

Yergin, Daniel and Joseph Stanislaw: The Commanding Heights: The Battle for the World Economy. Free Press. 2002

Zelmanovitz, Leonidas: The Ontology and Function of Money: The Philosophical Fundamentals of Monetary Institutions (Capitalist Thought: Studies in Philosophy, Politics, and Economics). Lexington Books 2015

ABOUT THE AUTHOR

Antony P. Mueller is a German professor of economics who currently teaches in Brazil. He is an associate scholar of the Ludwig von Mises Institute USA and a senior fellow of the American Institute for Economic Research. He obtained his doctorate at the Friedrich-Alexander University Erlangen-Nuremberg, Germany.

Contact:
antonymueller@gmx.com
See his Amazon author page:https://www.amazon.com/ANTONY-P.-MUELLER/e/B07BHF4RG8/ref=ntt_dp_epwbk_0

RELATED BOOKS

Beyond the State and Politics. Capitalism for the New Millennium. Amazon KDP 2018

ISBN-10: 1717773761
ISBN-13: 978-1717773760

Capitalism Beyond the State and Politics. Expanded textbook edition. Amazon KDP 2018

ISBN-10: 1717759890
ISBN-13: 978-1717759894

www.ingramcontent.com/pod-product-compliance
Lightning Source LLC
Chambersburg PA
CBHW031418210526
45464CB00005B/1936